Measuring Intangible Values

T0295791

This book explores the complex problem of how to measure the 'success' of social organizations, projects and activities. Whether improving a local situation, organizing a campaign around sustainability or assessing the intangible effects of perceived social benefits, currently we only have a very limited range of mechanisms for judging effectiveness. On the one hand, a market-driven logic demands that qualitative perceptions and experiences are quantified into simplified and numerically defined variables. On the other, community projects are left un-assessed, as one-off outcomes of local and situated processes that must somehow automatically 'make things better'. For academics, researchers and other professionals working in this field this has resulted in the deep frustration of not being able to assess the things that are most centrally important: higher human values such as integrity, trust, respect, equality and social justice.

Measuring Intangible Values argues that we can make shared social values – and their measurement – central to decisions about improving civil society. But because these social values are intangible, we need to develop ways of eliciting and validating them at the local level that can capture people's shared meanings across multiple goals and perspectives. We need to develop mechanisms for evaluating whether these values are met that use rigorous but also relevant measures. And we need to develop ways of doing this that are scalable, transferable and comparable across different kinds of organizations and fields of activity.

This book will be valuable for researchers in all social science disciplines which touch on human values, such as sociology, social psychology, human geography, social policy, architecture and planning, design and community studies.

Marie Harder is a China National Thousand Talents Professor at Fudan University, Shanghai, and the Founder and Head of the Values and Sustainability research group at the University of Brighton, UK.

Gemma Burford has been a Research Fellow in Sustainable Development at the University of Brighton, UK, and previously worked in Tanzania as Founder and Co-Director of the NGO Aang Serian ('House of Peace').

Routledge Studies in Sustainability

www.routledge.com/Routledge-Studies-in-Sustainability/book-series/RSSTY

Measuring Intangible Values

Rethinking How to Evaluate Socially
Beneficial Actions

Marie Harder and Gemma Burford

Routledge
Taylor & Francis Group
LONDON AND NEW YORK

from Routledge

First published 2019 by Routledge

2 Park Square, Milton Park, Abingdon, Oxfordshire OX14 4RN

52 Vanderbilt Avenue, New York, NY 10017

Routledge is an imprint of the Taylor & Francis Group, an informa business

First issued in paperback 2020

British Library Cataloguing-in-Publication Data
A catalogue record for this book is available from the British Library

Library of Congress Cataloging-in-Publication Data
A catalog record has been requested for this book

ISBN: 978-1-138-07958-8 (hbk)
ISBN: 978-0-367-50057-3 (pbk)

Typeset in Goudy
by Wearset Ltd, Boldon, Tyne and Wear

Contents

Figures

Tables

Acknowledgements

We would like to acknowledge all the contributors to this evolving work so far, noting that although some worked for longer periods and/or major strands, that it was only through the diversity of the contributions and perspectives, even of the short-term contributors, that we got to where we are today. Two particularly long-term contributors alongside Marie Harder and Gemma Burford were Elona Hoover and Firooz Firoozmand. Contributors mostly at the original ESDinds stage were: Arthur L Dahl, Tomas Hak, Dimity Podger, Georgia Piggot, Ismael Velasco, Cardiela Amézcua Luna, Svatava Janouskova, Martin Zahradnik, Poppy Villiers-Stuart, Daniel Truran, Alicia Jimenez, John Smith, Curtis Volk – and Julie Carter who kept us all organized. People who were instrumental in the ESDinds conceptualization, and thus its core premises, included Sylvia Karlsson, Victoria Thoressen, and Alan Atkisson. Short-term Brighton team members along the way included Dirk Book, Paul Hanna and Lee Stapleton for a few months each. Management at the University of Brighton that gave us space to survive, and sometimes thrive, were Andrew Lloyd and Stuart Laing. We would also like to acknowledge the University of Fudan, Shanghai, for providing the opportunity to publish this work in book form, and to Yanyan Huang for her assistance.

The work reported in this book includes original research, funded by the European Union's Seventh Framework Programme (Grant No. 212237) under the 'Research for the Benefit of Specific Groups: Civil Society Organizations' strand. The original EU project was known as ESDinds, running from January 2009 to March 2011, and all of the subsequent work builds directly on it. The sponsor had no involvement in the design or conduct of the research; in the preparation of the report; or in the decision to submit for publication. The work on legacy reported in this volume was funded by the Arts & Humanities Research Council AHRC grant: 'Starting from Values – Evaluating Intangible Legacies AH/L013142/1'. In this project, 'Starting from Values', we had the most amazing, diverse, creative collaborators outside of Brighton including Julian Brigstocke, Paula Graham, Sophia de Sousa, Andy Dearden, Ann Light, Theodore Zamenopoulos, Katerina Alexiou, Justine Gaubert, Colin Fosket, and Leila Downey. In the EU PERL schools project we additionally co-produced with many sub-groups of their large consortium. We would like to thank all of these people, as well as all those study participants we have not mentioned, for giving us so much of their time and effort.

Finally, we would like to thank Jos Boys, who took on the role of editor and critical friend in the development of this publication, and to Rebecca Brennan from Earthscan/Routledge for her support.

Some of this work has been published in earlier versions. We thank the relevant book and journal publications, as well as cited co-authors, for their permission to reuse, as follows:

Harder, M.K., Buford, G., and Hoover, E. (2013) 'What is Participation? Design Leads the Way to a Cross-Disciplinary Framework', *Design Issues*, 29(4) (Autumn), pp. 41–57. © 2013 by the Massachusetts Institute of Technology, adapted and reprinted by permission of the MIT Press.

Burford, G., Hoover, E., Stapleton, L., and Harder, M. (2016) 'An Unexpected Means of Embedding Ethics in Organizations: Preliminary Findings from Values-Based Evaluations', *Sustainability*, 8, p. 612. Permission to adapt reprint materials has been granted by MDPI, as part of its Open Access Policy.

Burford, G., Hoover, E., Velasco, I., Janoušková, S., Jimenez, A., Piggot, G., Podger, D., and Harder, M.K. (2013) 'Bringing the "Missing Pillar" into Sustainable Development Goals: Towards Inter-subjective Values-Based Indicators', *Sustainability*, 5(7), pp. 3035–3059. Permission to adapt reprint materials has been granted by MDPI, as part of its Open Access Policy.

Podger, D., Velasco, I., Amezcua Luna, C., Burford, G. and Harder, M.K. (2013) 'Can Values Be Measured? Significant Contributions from a Small Civil Society Organisation Through Action Research', *Action Research*, 11(1), pp. 8–30. By permission of SAGE Publications Ltd.

Harder, M.K., Velasco, I., and Burford, G. (2014) 'Reconceptualizing "Effectiveness" in Environmental Projects: Can We Measure Values-Related Achievements?' *Journal of Environmental Management*, 139, pp. 120–134. With thanks to Elsevier.

Introduction

This book explores the complex problem of how to measure the success of social organizations, projects and activities. Whether improving a local situation, organizing a campaign around sustainability or assessing the intangible effects of perceived social benefits, currently we only have a very limited range of mechanisms for judging effectiveness. On the one hand, a market-driven logic demands that qualitative perceptions and experiences are quantified into simplified and numerically defined variables, which are alien to the reality. On the other, community projects are left un-assessed, and considered un-assessable but with one-off outcomes of local and situated processes that must somehow automatically 'make things better'. This leaves us with public uncertainties about social and ethical values, and the projects based on them. It means that we are often left with a deeply unsatisfactory binary choice as the basis of our judgements; to choose between either an artificial scoring system or a random mix of intuition, opinion and 'common sense'. For academics, researchers, social entrepreneurs, civic society organizations and other professionals working in the social, voluntary and community sectors this has resulted in the deep frustration of not being able to assess the things that are most centrally important; things that are commonly related to higher human values such as integrity, trust, respect, equality and social justice. It produces a disconnect between what such individuals and organizations are trying to do, and the way this had to be articulated in funding bids and evaluation data and even in presentation of the work to a wider public. In effect, through lack of appropriate measures, workers in human values-based projects must live a half-lie.

The story told in this book, and the unfolding approach it describes, grew out of these frustrations with existing forms of monitoring and evaluation. The argument offered here is that we *can* make shared social values – and their measurement – central to decisions about improving civil society. But because these social values are intangible, we need to develop ways of eliciting and validating them at the local level that can capture people's shared meanings across multiple goals and perspectives. We need to develop mechanisms for evaluating whether these values are met; mechanisms that use rigorous but also relevant measures. These measures also need to 'work' for granting bodies and sponsors, giving them clarity about what had been achieved, and its resource-effectiveness. And we need to develop ways of doing this that are scalable, transferable and comparable across different kinds of organizations and fields of activity.

To do this, *Measuring Intangible Values: Rethinking How to Evaluate Socially Beneficial Actions* first sets the scene by looking at 'research through design' or RtD (Frayling 1993; Archer 1995). What is special about this approach is that it understands design as a process to produce artefacts and outcomes that can transform the world from its current state to an improved one. Such artefacts – in our case, participatory processes and tools – are seen as not just one-offs, being more about developing exemplars that enable transferable knowledge. As Durrant *et al.* put it:

> The term (RtD) has gained traction in many diverse fields of design, from fashion, for example, to human-computer interaction. Arguably, research through design is not a formal methodological approach with a particular epistemological basis. Instead, it is a foundational concept for approaching inquiry through the practice of design; and as a concept it has been subjected to multiple articulations and interpretations both by individuals and by institutions.
>
> (2017: 3)

For us, creative and collaborative approaches with iterative reflection have been central, also building on other open-ended methodologies that draw out emergent themes, rather than using pre-framed modes of enquiry. For example, we have also used grounded theory. However, because research through design remains an ambiguous and developing field, much debated and discussed (Zimmerman *et al.* 2007), we are also interested in how our work can help refine arguments and offer more consistent frameworks. Crucially the action research outlined in this book aims to show how such open-ended (and open-minded) approaches can also produce proper unitary validity that is comparable and generalizable; that is, with outcomes that can be measured. We will first show how explicit understandings of a group's shared intangible values can be enabled to emerge from local collectivities, through the design of a richly collaborative and co-development process. We will then go on to explain how to generate measurement indicators that grow out of those shared social values, and have unitary validity for everyone involved, and for the intended uses. Second, the book describes how this values-based framework has developed through time, learning from a variety of global action research projects and the many participants involved, so as to iteratively move towards more valid, community-led and locally empowering versions of the approach. Importantly this has been a learning journey for the researchers as much as the civil society organisations involved, since the research and development process has also been designed to be open-ended and exploratory. Here, we will draw out four key emergent themes:

i techniques for making intangible values explicit and measurable;
ii how the process of eliciting values is itself a powerful mechanism for organizational self-understanding and development;
iii what kinds of participatory methods enable the equitable engagement of every group member;
iv how to develop measures that meet robust validity criteria.

Finally, the book looks at three case studies in detail, to illustrate what such a values-based framework looks like in practice, and some of the diverse ways civil society organizations can use it. The book concludes with some ideas about future development.

In the current period, as global inequalities remain intractable and effective collective responses to climate change are becoming crucial, being able to articulate and measure intangible social values is increasingly vital. The United Nations 2030 Agenda for Sustainable Development (2015) highlights the importance of developing new measures of progress at societal levels – rather than relying on gross domestic product (GDP) as the sole indicator. The values-based approach developed here enables the effective generation of new measures, and new ways of enabling groups to design their own – valid – measures, in response to this challenge. It therefore aims to be part of the strongly developing global debate about how to both put shared social values at the centre of development, and how to have appropriate but also rigorous methods for driving social change.

This book is relevant to many different audiences, because the artificial divide between conventional 'business-based' evaluation methods and desired 'community-relevant' ones affects every level of society from governmental policy through professional and commercial organisations down to grassroots groups and initiatives. By offering a viable alternative approach to these limited models, through a developing narrative beginning from research through design methods that can act as a generator of debate and development, this book has much to contribute. It is of clear relevance to subjects such as sociology, social psychology, human geography, social policy, architecture and planning, design and community studies – indeed for any discipline that has an emphasis on community-engaged research – as well as to these and other subjects that deal with sustainability (a key theme in the development of a values-based approach), or which place an emphasis on action research. It also has a particular value for those interested in research through design methodologies, in suggesting ways of productively taking these methods forward. Whilst the book centres on developing a values-based evaluation model, the case studies and examples highlight its importance to, and direct connections with, these other disciplines and related investigations.

This book is also of crucial importance to grassroots and other civil society organisations (CSOs), because being able to measure intangible social values is of crucial importance to them. These include public service providers and non-governmental entities (NGOs), as well as values-based businesses such as social enterprises and not-for-profit companies. Whether these groups operate at a local, regional, national, international or global level, they can benefit and even be emancipated by exploring our increasingly refined approach, enabling social values to be elicited, validated, monitored and evaluated. Since this could relate to a major shift in how such organisations work and interact with other stakeholders, an improved understanding of how values-based approaches work will also appeal to business schools and to management studies, politics and economics; to public policy makers at local, national and international levels; and to commercial businesses and social enterprises that work in the area of public and social engagement. By taking a cross-disciplinary approach, the work builds on the power and importance of bringing together different perspectives on social issues. In addition, because the action research underpinning this book has a global range, it will be of interest to groups and individuals worldwide. Finally, it opens doors to measuring values based on aspects of interest to all those trying to measure such programmes.

Chapter outline

In keeping with the frameworks outlined above, this book is organized as a developmental journey (as it indeed was for everyone involved); trying to make explicit the learning that developed *en route*, as much as for the researchers as for the CSOs. The first part outlines the processes the initial EU-funded project went through in co-designing an initial values-based framework, to reveal how approaches and understandings changed and deepened considerably through that time, particularly in the case study testing. The second part explores three key emergent themes: the shift from a focus on 'just measuring' to a more holistic framework for drawing out and crystallising values; the generation of appropriate participatory approaches, both in the research project consortium and in the case study trials; and a fuller analysis of validity considerations for measuring intangible social values. The final part explores three case studies in greater depth, to show how a values-based approach can support diverse intentions and requirements, adapt to the specifics of each civil society organization and context and begin to address emergent issues that grew out of the original project.

As with the action research on which it is based, this book is therefore organized as an unfolding story where the lessons learned through each iteration can and do deeply inform and enrich the approach; and with the intention that the reader is also invited to engage discursively with the content. The overall aim is not to describe or argue over existing power relationships in organisations or society, but to provide useable, easily understandable tools for individuals and groups to make ethically sound and socially beneficial decisions with and for their communities – through understanding and taking measures of indicators of their values.

Part I Designing a values-based framework

Why values?

This chapter introduces the concept of shared social values – related to concepts such as trust, respect and justice – within a group; and the associated problem of intangibility 'versus' measurability. It argues for a better and more explicit understanding of shared group values, their central importance to community and public projects and initiatives and the necessity of finding ways to capture and have appropriate measures for these values. It proposes that to do this requires the abandonment of models that attempt to reductively pre-define values variables; instead aiming for approaches that can accept fuzziness, whilst holding onto validity. To do this, we address first what we mean by value; second, the issue of whose values are being articulated; third, the relationship between values and their evaluation; and finally, how the seeming problem of intangible values versus measurement can be powerfully reframed.

Articulating values, designing processes

In this chapter, an introductory values-based framework is outlined. We describe the original process used to develop an overall set of generalizable values headings and their associated indicators, as well as the design of a development process based on participatory, dynamic and emergent mechanisms for generating and then validating those values as shared. We then outline how this was developed out of research through design, and related approaches. This chapter also demonstrates the iterative nature of the action research, as the research team continually learned from participating groups, so that – as the next chapter will show – many aspects of the value statements, participatory processes and assumed outcomes, were substantially changed or replaced.

Developing a values-based approach: the case of Echeri

An initial field project (2010) was with Echeri Consultores, a non-profit organization based in Michoacan, Mexico, working with youngsters to reconnect them to their local environment via values education based on the Earth Charter. This chapter explores a detailed field-testing of an early toolkit version of the approach. It focuses on how the academic researchers and local organization worked together, and the diversity of non-verbal methods used with the children and youth to elicit values and measure effectiveness. Most crucially it shows that not only did groups adapt the values-based approach to their own requirements, but they also began to use it productively for a variety of purposes. For example, the approach became a means to debate and respond to differences in values across an organization and to produce transformational change, both as individuals and systemically. In addition, in some cases the toolkit enabled capacity building – building self-esteem, confidence and new abilities to self-develop ways of capturing 'measures' of values-based achievements and being able to communicate these more widely. This chapter also shows the ways in which, as the group came to make the approach their own, some core research questions for the whole framework were reshaped.

Part II   Key themes in measuring intangible social values

Issues in making values tangible

The insights enabled by working with Echeri led to new questions. How should values-in-action become pooled, from the existing values and indicator lists? How did the framing of values and indicators need to be redesigned so that group and individual participants did not need to stay within the 'bounds' of selecting and adapting values from a list; but actually adapted and redefined these values to their own specific situation, the ways they saw them relating to each other, and thus also generating alternative forms of measurement. This chapter outlines the lessons learned, and the issues that were raised in attempting to make values tangible.

Designing processes: the criticality of deep participation

Our work in the field led to a need to critically investigate our participation processes beyond the immediate demands of, and lessons learned from, each individual CSO project evaluation. What would a participation framework look like, that whilst starting from designing evaluation methods suited to particular civil society organizations, would enable us to generate a robust, and more generally useful model? Could the outcomes from our case study trials inform this larger aim? This chapter explores what such a method for comparing and contrasting different evaluations would look like, based on their depth, breadth, scope and outcomes. In particular, it aims to capture how to measure and communicate levels of deeply engaged participation – increasingly recognizable as a central variable.

Values and validity

One of the key perceived problems with articulating intangible shared values is the assumption that these are always vague, personal and not measurable. In this chapter we want to deal with the issue of validity in a rigorous manner. We therefore examine different kinds of validity, and discuss their relevance to the values-based approach argued for in this book. The aim is to demonstrate not only that intangible values can be measured in ways that have validity, but also that conventional ways of understanding validity – and the standardised processes through which these are implemented – are deeply problematic in making invisible action that is centrally about community and social change.

Part III Putting a values-based framework into practice

Sustainability and business ethics

The original EU-funded ESDinds project included work with eight organizations across seven countries, with the aim of facilitating organisations to evaluate themselves in a manner which they considered valid and relevant, centred on sustainability issues. This chapter outlines an exploratory study that tried to make sense of the anecdotal impacts that we later recorded from our project on the organisations themselves, particularly around issues of business ethics. This is because our focus on intangible shared social values is inherently about ethics, and so this constitutes a crucial area of debate and discussion in conversations around transitions to sustainability more widely. The study draws out how individuals and organizations could become more ethical, through using our values-based approach.

Mapping social legacies

A core requirement for many organizations is to map effects and actions beyond the life of a particular project or initiative. This is likely to be a formal demand from funders, but is also vital to community actions having a longevity and powerfulness. This chapter describes a case study of using our approach to not only map the legacies that groups had initially defined, but also, through cross-group collaboration, to generate additional, and previously intangible legacy aims and measures. This was through an innovative Arts and Humanities Research Council (AHRC) funded initiative that investigated how to make equal and effective community-academic partnerships.

Towards sustainable behaviour change in schools

The final case study explored in this book has a focus on Education for Sustainable and Responsible Living (EfSRL) teaching in schools, and how this might be better achieved. This was an international project that aimed to inspire students to identify their own values, and recognize and strengthen the skills necessary to ensure they survive and thrive in the 21st century. We were particularly interested to work with students and their teachers in order to move beyond current gaps between knowledge delivery in school curricula, and actual action and behavior change by individuals and institutions. The chapter outlines the development and prototyping of a set of toolkits to enable a process of both eliciting shared intangible values around sustainability and social responsibility, and generating associated action statements.

Conclusion: what happens when values are central

The concluding chapter explores the many lessons we have learnt along the way and some wider implications of the approach outlined throughout this book. It suggests that the learning acquired has resulted from careful attendance to shoots and offshoots of the original objective: 'How can we help civil society groups find a way to measure and communicate the achievements that are of worth to them?' It shows what can be achieved when there is no preconception of what the solution would look like; when the aim is be without a bias for specific disciplinary approaches and accompanying frameworks; and when the process is one of iteratively reflecting, consulting with partners, exploring in practice, and observing linked findings. It thus investigates not only the various project outcomes themselves, but also the implications for values-based and related research more generally.

The team behind *Measuring Intangible Values* are committed to opening up rigorous ways of eliciting and measuring shared social values in organizations. By being enabled to measure things that have not previously been measured – such as trust, empowerment and integrity – a values-based approach also begins to communicate a new voice for society. Being able to explicitly discuss a shared vocabulary for organisations from local to national and even global levels that go beyond directly monetary or performance assessments enables social values and ethics to take a more central place in decision-making and transformational social action. The book gives examples of the kinds of impacts this is producing, such as groups offering new types of measures to funders, and the funders in turn using these to assess group effectiveness. This suggests that finding ways to measure intangible values is crucial for improving societal decision-making about more socially equitable and sustainable futures. In addition, both the values-based framework itself, and the iterative methods through which it developed, can open up new opportunities for critical and creative exchange, for constructive interdisciplinary working, and for accessing potentially rich sources of new knowledge at the overlaps, gaps and inconsistencies of different conceptual frameworks. By sharing our approach, experiences and lessons learnt, this book aims to be part of an on-going process of engagement, debate and further research.

References

Archer, B. (1995) 'The Nature of Research', *Co-Design*, (January), pp. 6–13.

Durrant, A. C., Vines, J., Wallace, J., and Yee, J. S. R. (2017) 'Research Through Design: Twenty-First Century Makers and Materialities', *Design Issues*, 33(3) (Summer), pp. 3–10.

Frayling, C. (1993) 'Research in Art and Design', *Royal College of Art Research Papers*, 1(1), pp. 1–5.

United Nations General Assembly (2015) *Transforming Our World: the 2030 Agenda for Sustainable Development* Retrieved from https://sustainabledevelopment.un.org/post2015/transformingourworld.

Zimmerman, J., Forlizzi, J., and Evenson, S. (2007) 'Research Through Design as a Method for Interaction Design in Human–Computer Interaction'. In *Conference on Human Factors in Computing Systems*. New York: ACM Press.

Part 1

Designing a values-based framework

1   Why values?

This chapter introduces the concept of shared social group values – human values related to concepts such as trust, respect, integrity and justice – and the problem of intangibility 'versus' measurability. It argues for a better and more explicit understanding of social values, their central importance to community and public projects and initiatives and the necessity of finding ways to capture and have appropriate and measurable indicators for these values. It proposes that to do this requires the abandonment of models that attempt to reductively pin down social variables; instead aiming for approaches that can accept fuzziness, whilst holding onto validity.

Unfortunately, traditional approaches to developing evaluation indicators usually start from the question 'what can be measured, using established methods or data sets?' – framing the creation of relevant indicators primarily as a technical issue, rather than a political or ethical one. By contrast, our values-based approach starts by asking 'what should be measured?' This chapter outlines how it has been possible to develop a generalizable framework for social values – based on what people think, feel, do and say – that can then become locally contextualized through group collaboration, and where, crucially, measurements are created by the groups themselves. To do this, we need to address first, what we mean by value; second, the issue of whose values are being articulated; third, the relationship between values and their evaluation; and finally, how the seeming problem of intangible value *versus* measurement can be powerfully reframed.

First, what do we mean by value? 'Values' have been adopted by innumerable civil society organisations, governments, public providers and businesses worldwide as a way of articulating their goals, particularly for ethical and sustainable practices. There is no universally accepted theoretical definition of values (Harder *et al.* 2014). An attempt to summarize and clarify the concept in social science literature identified 180 different definitions of 'value' (Horáková 2005). Influential versions include Kluckhohn's description of value as 'a conception, explicit or implicit, distinctive of an individual or characteristic of a group, of the desirable, which influences the selection from available modes, means and ends of action' (1951: 39); whilst Rokeach explained it as follows:

> A value is an enduring belief that a specific mode of conduct or end-state of existence is personally or socially preferable to an opposite or converse mode of conduct or end-state of existence. A value system is an enduring organization of beliefs concerning preferable modes of conduct or end-states of existence along a continuum of relative importance.
>
> (1973: 5)

In our work, when we speak of values, we mean 'principles or standards of behaviour: one's judgement of what is important in life' as defined by the Oxford Dictionary. Values make up who we are and they represent what we stand for as people and as organisations; they are a key driver to how we behave. In developing a value-based framework, then, we have defined values to be enduring beliefs about which kinds of behaviour and situations are good or bad, and which ones are centrally important to individuals and groups. Enduring means that these values are relatively stable and don't change from one day to the next – although of course they can be influenced by, and adapted through, our changing attitudes and contexts.

Our values relate to whatever is *valuable* to us as individuals, organisations, communities or nations – the things that give our lives some meaning. Some may value material wealth and improvements that happen to be easy to measure. Others value things that are less tangible, and related to concepts like honesty, integrity, justice, courage, respect or community spirit that are often called moral, spiritual, higher and ethical values. Whilst material aspects, such as money, can be easily counted and quantified, these intangible aspects – the value of values – are much harder to capture. How do you know you are doing well when goals are intangible? How do you measure trustworthiness, love, self-discipline, friendliness or patience? If your goal is to empower youth, increase social cohesion or promote democratic decision-making, how do you know when this has been achieved? This is what our action research set out to investigate.

Whose values?

A connected series of fundamental questions concerns *whose* values are being articulated. How and by whom are a project's beliefs and activities described and measured? Despite the substantial increase in the popularity of participatory methods for decision-making and for evaluation, funders still have the power of framing what is important about the activities they support (Burford *et al.* 2013). As Bamberger puts it, 'donors' information priorities and evaluation methodologies continue to exert considerable influence on how evaluation is practiced and used' (2000: 96). This remains particularly true in the global South (Springett 2003). Mismatches between what a donor wishes to evaluate and what the recipient organization regards as important can become highly problematic. Ebrahim (2003) reports on the tendency of donor appraisals to focus on easily measurable and quantifiable outputs, such as the number of schools built, trees planted or hectares of land irrigated, while neglecting more ambiguous and less tangible changes in social and political processes. In particular, bilateral donor agencies (government or non-profit organisations based in one country providing aid to other countries) often rely on logical framework analysis (LFA or 'logframes'), a method that entails constructing a matrix of the project's objectives, expected results, and indicators to be used in measuring progress towards those results.

The LFA approach has been criticized by Edwards and Hulme (1996) for overemphasizing short-term, quantitative targets and promoting 'accountancy' over 'accountability'. Ebrahim (2003) reports widespread concern among civil society organizations that as a result, donors tend to reward discrete, product-based approaches to development, while penalizing innovative process-based approaches with the potential to generate sustainable changes in behaviour. Civil society organizations are often pressured to develop onerous monitoring and evaluation systems that, while satisfying donor demands for information, are perceived to be of little relevance for their own internal decision-making and learning. This can lead to anger, insecurity and a paperwork burden that reduces the time available for core programme activities, leading to deep disillusionment about evaluation (Crishna 2007) and, potentially, even a *decrease* in effectiveness. While the situation is varied across different places, agencies and fields of study, there remains a strong tendency towards an evaluation agenda that requires only 'evidence of outcome achievement' (Fleming and Easton 2010).

This deeply problematic situation is not merely about a mismatch in what counts as core values between donor and recipient. It is clear that donors, too, are frustrated by their inability to measure the things that really matter. The philanthropic sector also struggles with evaluating itself, with finding ways of understanding whether its work is making a difference (Ford Foundation 2011). The CEO of the Vancouver Foundation has criticized the trend towards attempting to apply a 'return on investment' model to the act of giving, and to quantify the impact of charitable donations using standardized metrics (Wightman 2010). This is because – as with CSOs and other community groups – the benefits from given actions can also be amorphous and difficult to measure, and may take several years to be fully realized.

It is this very intangibility, that makes the articulation and assessment of values so hard. How then can we move to a still rigorous evaluation framework that is designed to capture dimensions relating to 'higher' ethical/spiritual values such as equality or empowerment, rather than the rigidity conventionally required for enabling comparability and generalizability?

Measuring intangibles

The notion of value and its assessment lies at the very heart of judging how effective an organization or project has been (Burford *et al.* 2012). Values thus need to be linked to measurable performance indicators. But there is often also a set of implicit values built into the methodology of the evaluation itself that will determine which variables are worth assessing, and what their relevant indicators are. Whilst rigorous evaluation design and implementation methods are applied to make sure measurements or assessments carried out are faithful representations of the variables selected, there is a crucial question about whether these chosen variables and indicators properly represent the reference values in the first place.

This need for improved evaluation tools for the values-based work of civil society organisations was the main driver for our two-year European-funded research programme to develop values-based indicators (ESDinds 2009–2011) which will be described in more detail in the next two chapters of this section. The project involved a consortium of two university research groups and four civil society organisations broadly concerned with values and sustainable development. The consortium members felt that intangible, values-related impacts of their sustainability work, which they could 'feel instinctively' as key to the success of their work but could not define concisely or illustrate with rigorous data, were omitted from evaluations and hence overlooked by donors because they were perceived to be impossible to measure.

Some recognized that, in the current financial climate, their very survival might depend on their ability to convince donors of such wider achievements and potential. Others felt the under-appreciation of values-based work was generally a reason that 'gross domestic product' (GDP) economics was failing, and saw critical importance in articulating their own core values in terms of measurable indicators and outcome data. It is unsurprising that values-based aspects of CSO work have been considered 'intangible' and eluded evaluation for so long, because CSOs themselves may often be unable to define these aspects in terms familiar to evaluators. For example, many CSOs do not distinguish between outcomes, processes and stakeholder perspectives, or between formative and summative evaluations. They may also consider several overlapping outcomes or processes as 'dynamic clusters' rather than delineating them cleanly, which makes targeting for specific evaluation very difficult. Conversely, CSOs are usually clear about whether a project was 'good' or 'bad' according to their own ethos, even if they have difficulty articulating the reasons.

A central element of the ESDinds work came to be called WeValue, to give an easily understandable title to the evaluation toolkits and participatory processes being developed. This was supported by the ESDinds Consortium (all the partners) who came together to address this crucial problem that conventional evaluation methodologies are failing to measure the intangible, values-related aspects of projects, of which they are the very heart. In an environment of fierce competition for limited funds, in which an organization's very survival can depend on its ability to convince donors of its achievements and potential, the CSO partners wanted to find a way of being able to understand, articulate and measure whatever it is that they value most. They also acknowledged that this ambitious goal would not be achieved by giving lip service to 'processes', while maintaining a focus on counting numbers of trees, workshops or participants. Rather, it would demand a radical rethinking of evaluation methodology.

The next step for the ESDinds Consortium was to develop a preliminary set of values-based indicators, with the aim of framing a common and shared vocabulary to discuss and evaluate some of the less tangible dimensions of their projects (Burford *et al.* 2012). Of course, the initial difficulty is the assumed indefinability of values as against, say, costs and benefits. Our first attempts to measure human values, the mysterious and intangible entities that conventional evaluators have overlooked, began with an exploration of what already existed in this field. This showed that existing often-cited examples such as the Rokeach Value Survey were problematic. This values classification instrument was developed in the 1970s, based on a rank ordering scaling of 36 values (Rokeach 1973). Like other values-linked approaches, Rokeach assumes that values 'transparently' produce their own indicators. It is also framed by the uncritical belief that there are a limited number of values which are universal for all cultures. Any cross-cultural differences are then dealt with only as a difference in the hierarchical ordering of values. Researchers analysing the results are then seen as 'objectively' capable of make inferences about the values held. Yet, when we talked about this with our partners, the CSOs involved in the Consortium found such value-words difficult to interpret cleanly enough to rank, even with considerable discussion. The inherent problem with Rokeach-based approaches in assuming values as directly approachable entities, and asking people to evaluate items such as 'accomplishment', 'love' and 'equality' (whether by ranking or rating), does not explore their understanding, and multiple interpretations, of these general terms. The same word may mean different things to different people, so discussion of values in a cultural vacuum can lead to lack of validity (Schlater and Sontag 1994). What then, were productive and concrete ways of tackling these difficulties?

Eliciting shared values

As noted above, we began by reviewing various approaches to the measurement of values, which derive research instruments to generate and shape data based on existing theories, that is, start from an already defined framework and then develop variables and relationships from there. We took the converse approach, using a grounded theory approach (Dey 1999; Charmaz 2006). This is a means for generating theory from data during the process of conducting research, and where themes emerge, rather than being pre-defined. This also meant that, like any form of action research, there is a productive tension between acknowledging the desirability of scientific rigor, on the one hand, and remaining flexible to the diverse needs and expectations of participating communities, on the other (Peterson 2010). So whilst it was important to understand what types of evidence would be required in order to demonstrate in a convincing way the validity of conclusions drawn from a project evaluation, we also recognized that framing what counted as evidence should start from the civil society organizations themselves.

Alongside this, ran a pragmatic need for usability that took into consideration the availability of human and financial resources in different contexts. So, for example, whilst academic researchers might insist upon the use of multiple methodologies, systematic cross-checks, and extensive pre-testing to maintain the structural and substantive validity of questionnaires and other instruments, we wanted an assessment system that was not so time-consuming as to be impracticable or burdensome. We felt it is imperative to avoid situations such as those described by Crishna (2007) in which complex and inappropriate monitoring and evaluation systems actually detract from core project activities.

A very useful contribution to this debate has been made by Cox *et al.* (2007) with the concept of 'fitness for purpose'. He defines this as meaning that the research addresses a problem that is important to society; that the purpose of the study, and the research question, are clearly defined; that the chosen method(s) can answer the research question and meet the purpose of the study; and that the methodology is theoretically and ethically legitimate. If all of these five criteria are met, the research can be described as fit for purpose, regardless of whether or not it also meets the validity criteria that might be imposed by a specific academic field.

Contemporary evaluation literature describes several interrelated theoretical approaches and practical strategies that can be drawn on to develop an evaluation framework for such intangible aspects of CSO work. First, we felt it was essential to give due consideration to process evaluation (e.g. Ellis and Hogard 2006; Hogard 2008) rather than focusing exclusively on outcome evaluation. By this, we mean that the processes through which CSOs work are often as important as the results of their activities. Thus a values-based methodology needed to consider not just concepts about what is important, but also how these are articulated through practices.

Second, we wanted our own approach to be based on principles of participatory evaluation (e.g. Crishna 2007; Springett 2003). We felt that these were indispensable in our localized contexts, as external evaluators rarely understand the CSO perspective sufficiently to identify specific intangibles for evaluation. This meant that it was essential for evaluation processes to be co-designed with our partners. Finally, we wanted an approach based on the principle that an evaluation should be judged on its usefulness to its intended users. Called utilisation-focused evaluation, and developed by Michael Quinn Patton (2008), this frames the evaluator's job as not making decisions independently of the intended users, but as a facilitator of decision making amongst the people who will use the findings of the evaluation to improve their own situation. This requires an iterative and flexible approach based on reflection and 'feedback loops' (Flowers 2010). In addition, the growing literature on process use (e.g. Crohn and Birnbaum 2010; Holte-McKenzie, Forde, and Theobald 2006) emphasizes that the utility of evaluation lies not only in the findings themselves, but also in processes that cause CSO staff to engage in systematic reflection on their projects and sometimes lead to changes in perspective. As we will show later, the ability of a value-based framework to enable such transformations became a central element of the project as it developed.

We suggest that this work has led to a fundamentally new framework for understanding human values, their operationalization and their measurement. Values, from this perspective, can neither be described as cosmically objective – that is, universally 'true', independently of the facts of certain shared human desires – nor as relating only to the subjective emotional states of individuals. Rather, we see them as depending on human desires that are shared across the species, or at least within a group culture, and therefore have 'inter-subjective objectivity' (Colvert 2007). Values can therefore by understood as categories that are *assigned* to behaviour and attitudes through subjective, personal acts of interpretation, rather than as concrete, mutually independent entities. Through a process of dialogue in which different people in a group share and compare their individual perspectives, collective – or, more precisely, inter-subjective – understandings of values can be achieved. The next chapter outlines in more details the development of this approach as a set of value statements and indicators; and the beginning design of participatory processes through which these can be both made explicit and measurable.

The advantages of such an approach for civil society organizations are three-fold. First, values-based indicators should enable CSOs, donors and beneficiaries to define and clearly verbalize what were previously merely *implicit* program objectives and goals, based on human values, which resonate with group members at a deep level. This requires a crystallization process – a rather significant and elusive step in its own right – which can generate a profound transformation of individuals, interpersonal relationships and organizational culture. Second, the indicators provide a positive view of the values baseline at the time of evaluation. Where problems are identified, they facilitate the question 'What is missing?' rather than 'What's gone wrong?' – aiding stakeholders to understand the root causes, without blaming or shaming individuals. Third, they can assist in strategic planning – helping CSOs (as well as donors) to prioritize the activities that bring their vision and mission to life, while eliminating those that are too amorphous, ineffective or distracting. The implications of adopting values-based indicators at a societal level are greater still. As Henshaw (2006) has observed, the process of measurement not only reflects, but contributes to *defining* what is important to an organization or a society: having the goal of successfully meeting evaluation indicators will itself affect behaviour. By defining a system through which intangible human values can be both expressed and measured in a useful way, we can make these more explicitly central to how groups define and evaluate themselves; break down the unspoken taboos against bringing these values into formal academic and policy arenas; and in particular, bring such 'intangible' values into the ranking of nations in a 'post-GDP' new economic paradigm.

Emergent processes: learning from research through design

It is the underpinning argument of this book that civil society organizations need both richer and more robust evaluation measures for what they do. For example, a sustainable development project needs more than conventional indicators, like the number of trees planted. If their project empowers a community, establishes a trusting work environment or improves social and economic justice, how would that be known? Which of these values-based indicators are important to capture? Which values contribute to sustainable development outcomes? Which of the 'espoused' values in an organisation's mission statement are actually in use in practice? If CSOs knew the answers to these questions, they could plan their activities better, optimising outcomes from their limited funding. This work grew out of the belief that CSOs, working together with specialised researchers to help crystallise these issues, could co-design and test a values-based framework. The original ESDinds project had the aim of developing toolkits and processes potentially useful to diverse values-based organisations, using co-production processes for working together. Our CSOs and academics were equal partners, grounded in the acknowledgement from the start that the goal could not be achieved if either dominated, because the source of the practical knowledge needed was embedded in CSO practice and not understood by the academics, and the rigorous methods needed to formalize it would come from the skills of the academics that the CSOs did not have. As already outlined, this led the research team to next explore possible collaborative action frameworks that were emergent, open-ended, participatory and creative, whilst still framed by rigorous approaches and methods. As outlined in the introduction, one central jumping off point for this was the research through design literature.

The concept of research through design (RtD) is widely recognised as originating in Christopher Frayling's threefold classification of research in art and design, which aimed to differentiate between research *about* the subject (the most generally assumed relationship, including history and theory of design for example) with the kinds of research that designers themselves undertake, often in relation to a specific project, but also more widely, for example in analysing and creatively responding to societal problems. He termed these three variations research *into* art and design, research *for* art and design and research *through* art and design (1993). A similar threefold classification of art and design research has also been described by Bruce Archer, who distinguished research *about* practice, research *for the purposes of* practice and research *through* practice (1995). His understanding of research through design has much in common with established definitions of action research, such as the 'Manifesto on Transformation of Knowledge Creation' signed by 60 advisory editors of the journal *Action Research* (Bradbury-Huang 2009). The importance of generating a wider transformative impact (described in the 'Manifesto' as 'meaning and relevance beyond an immediate context in support of the flourishing of persons, communities, and the wider ecology';

ibid.: 98) is also echoed in other literature on research through design, especially in its application to human–computer interaction. Zimmerman and Forlizzi (2008) for example, focus on the transformative role of design research in
addressing difficult societal problems – understanding RtD as the making of
artefacts intended to effect change, i.e. to transform a problematic or undesirable current situation into a preferred future situation.

Research through design, then, can be differentiated from conventional
research in both the sciences and the arts by being grounded in the specific epis-
temology of design described by Cross (1999) as an ongoing process of model-
ling and synthesis. For him, the knowledge fields of design centre on the
man-made world, on using imagination and practical experimentation as core
ways of knowing and exploring that world (rather than, for example, scientific
rationality or objectivity). In addition to being distinct from other types of
research, research through design is also a specific type of activity within the
design disciplines – one that centres strategic rather than particular or just
project-based aims. Designed activities and 'things' may seem to start from
meeting specific needs, but the intended overall goals in research through design
approaches are their contribution to knowledge and contribution to society.
The emphasis for RtD, then, is on complex or 'wicked' problems (Buchanan
1995; Farrell and Hooker 2013). Rather than more conventional design intentions around making improvements to a current situation, research through
design methods involve developing, for example, new processes and methods;
future research agendas, often in the form of a 'nascent theory of the near future'
(Zimmerman and Forlizzi 2008: 44); and the application of design to new areas.
Such an approach seemed capable of richly informing the processes we were
starting with our academic and civil society organization partners to develop
measurement frameworks for intangible social values.

However, as van de Weijer *et al.* (2014) point out (focusing particularly on
reviewing RtD within architecture) there is considerable variation and contestation in translating research through design as a concept or attitude into specific forms of knowledge production or underpinning methodologies:

> A brief literature review reveals that many authors conceive of research and
> design as antithetical. In discussing the characteristics of scientific research
> on the one hand and/or of design on the other, these authors focus on the
> differences between both. [...] Most commonly, standards of good research
> are deemed to include a systematic process, rigor, transparency, communi-
> cability, repeatability, validity, and originality. [...] Design activities, on the
> other hand, are evaluated according to other principles, which are harder to
> generalize because they depend on the project brief, the scale, contemporary
> professional norms, the client, and other factors. These activities are char-
> acterized by subjective, decisive key moments that exemplify the import-
> ance of tacit knowledge in making rapid progress working on a complex
> project.
>
> (2014: 3–4)

In addition, design is most often seen as a specific answer to a particular problem; research as going from empirical findings to generally valid statements and theories. Here, though, we agree with van de Weijers *et al.* that 'research and design can be brought together in a productive, investigative practice as a valid form of scientific practice' (ibid.: 4), such that the work here both moves towards new kinds of rigorous and valid knowledge (processes and tools) and can 'talk back' to RtD about developing more effective and appropriate methodologies. As Mottram and Rust explain, research through design can provide 'a location or focus [i.e. an applied process to be studied in a scientific context] upon which to direct questions, [...] a means of generating data, a site for testing propositions, for engaging individuals and communities, or for reflecting on theories and methods' (2008: 135).

The strength of such a design-centred approach lies in the fact that the research agenda is defined by the willingness of co-partners to function as 'explorers in the borderlands' between and beyond established academic disciplines. What this means in practice is the investigation of successive research questions as they emerge organically from the central design problem – in our case, the creation of a values-based evaluation framework – without prejudice as to their disciplinary roots (or lack of them). In order to be successful, this approach itself demands the enactment of certain values –including flexibility, openness to different ways of knowing, and a deep level of mutual understanding and trust between academic and community co-researchers (Burford *et al.* 2013). By building an atmosphere of trust, open-endedness and collaboration, community partners can be empowered to bring their tacit, intangible and praxis-embedded knowledges to the metaphorical drawing board; and academic partners can be encouraged to open their eyes, hearts and minds to the validity and usefulness of such knowledges, and to build on these strengths. This is also a fundamental principle that can be drawn from the co-design literature, in which all partners are acknowledged from the outset as 'experts of their experiences' (Sleeswijk Visseret *et al.* 2005; Steen, Manschot and De Koning 2011).

In starting from the RtD approach described above, it was also natural to make good use of many of the overlapping knowledge fields, such as established grounded approach guidelines for collecting and analysing data, and action research principles for ensuring deep learning between partners. We also took note of emancipatory action research as defined by Grundy (1987: 154) as research that 'promotes emancipatory praxis in the participating practitioners; that is, it promotes a critical consciousness which exhibits itself in political as well as practical action to promote change'. We also aimed to align with empowerment evaluation as outlined by Fetterman and Wandersman (2005), which involves principles of collaboration, self-determination, capacity building, equality, and partners acting as critical friends. Empowerment evaluation can be distinguished from related approaches, such as collaborative, participatory and utilization-focused evaluation, by its explicit focus on catalysing political and social change (Patton 2008). All of these share, then, the characteristics of empirical research aimed towards advancing emancipatory knowledge, and what has been called 'postdisciplinarity' knowledge. The next chapter outlines how these initial steps were first translated into actual values statements and frameworks that could be tested with civil society organisations in real contexts; and then describes the learning from all involved – the groups, the consortium and the research team.

References

Archer, B. (1995) 'The Nature of Research', *Co-Design, Interdisciplinary Journal of Design*, 2, pp. 6–13.

Bamberger, M. (2000). 'The Evaluation of International Development Programs: A View from the Front', *American Journal of Evaluation*, 21(1), pp. 95–102.

Bradbury-Huang, H. (2009) What Is Good Action Research? Why the Resurgent Interest? *Action Research*, 8(1), pp. 93–109.

Buchanan, R. (1995) 'Wicked Problems in Design Thinking'. In Margolin, V. and Buchanan, R. (Eds.) *The Idea of Design*. Cambridge, MA: MIT Press.

Burford, G., Valasco, I., Janoušková, S., Zahradnik, M., Hak, T., Podger, D., Piggot, G., and Harder, M. K. (2012) 'Field Trials of a Novel Toolkit for Evaluating "Intangible" Values-Related Dimensions Of Projects', *Evaluation and Program Planning*, 36(1), pp. 1–14.

Burford, G., Hoover, E., Velasco, I., Janoušková, S., Jimenez, A., Piggot, G., Podger, D., and Harder, M. K. (2013) 'Bringing the "Missing Pillar" into Sustainable Development Goals: Towards Intersubjective Values-Based Indicators', *Sustainability*, 5(7), pp. 3035–3059.

Charmaz, C. (2006) *Constructing Grounded Theory: A Practical Guide Through Qualitative Analysis*. London: Sage

Colvert, G. (2007) 'Back to Nature: Aquinas and Ethical Naturalism', *LYCEUM*, 13(2) (Spring), pp. 1–63.

Cox, T., Karanika, M., Griffiths, A. and Houdmont, J. (2007) 'Evaluating Organizational Level Work Stress Interventions: Beyond Traditional Methods', *Work & Stress*, 21(4), pp. 348–362.

Crishna, B. (2007) 'Participatory Evaluation (I) – Sharing Lessons from Fieldwork in Asia', *Child Care Health and Development*, 33(3), pp. 217–223.

Crohn, K. and Birnbaum, M. (2010). 'Environmental Education Evaluation: Time to Reflect, Time for Change', *Evaluation and Program Planning*, 33(2), pp. 155–158.

Cross, N. (1999) 'Design Research: A Disciplined Conversation', *Design Issues*, 15(2) (Summer), pp. 5–10.

Dey, I. (1999) *Grounding Grounded Theory: Guidelines for Qualitative Inquiry*. London: Academic Press.

Ebrahim, A. (2003) 'Accountability in Practice: Mechanisms for NGOs', *World Development*, 31(5), pp. 813–829.

Edwards, M. and Hulme, D. (1996) 'Too Close for Comfort? The Impact of Official Aid on Nongovernmental Organizations', *World Development*, 24(6), pp. 961–973.

Ellis, R. and Hogard, E. (2006) 'The Trident: A Three-Pronged Method for Evaluating Clinical, Social and Educational Innovations', *Evalution*, 12(3) (July), pp. 372–383.

Farrell, R. and Hooker, C. (2013) 'Design, Science and Wicked Problems', *Design Studies*, 34, pp. 681–705.

Fetterman, D. M. and Wandersman, A. (2005) (Eds.), *Empowerment Evaluation Principles in Practice*. New York: Guilford Publications.

Fleming, M. L. and Easton, J. (2010) 'Building Environmental Educators' Evaluation Capacity Through Distance Education', *Evaluation and Programme Planning*, 33(2) (May), pp. 172–177. doi: 10.1016/j.evalprogplan.2009.07.007.

Flowers, A. B. (2010) 'Blazing an Evaluation Pathway: Lessons Learned from Applying Utilization-Focused Evaluation to a Conservation Education Program', *Evaluation and Program Planning*, 33(2), pp. 165–171.

Ford Foundation. (2011) *Our Approach to Impact Assessment and Learning*. Retrieved from www.fordfoundation.org/impact/approach.

Frayling, C. (1993) 'Research in Art and Design', *Royal College of Art Research Papers*, 1(1), pp. 1–5.

Grundy, S. (1987) *Curriculum: Product or Praxis?* Lewes: Falmer Press.

Harder, M. K., Velasco, I., Burford, G., Podger, D., Janoušková, S., Piggot, G., and Hoover, E. (2014) 'Reconceptualising "Effectiveness" in Environmental Projects: Can We Measure Values-Related Achievements?' *Journal Of Environmental Management*, 139, pp. 120–134.

Henshaw, J. M. (2006) 'Does Measurement Measure up? How Numbers Reveal and Conceal the Truth'. In *Measurement in Business: What Gets Measured Gets Done*. Johns Hopkins University Press: Baltimore, MD, pp. 55–65.

Hogard, E. (2008) 'Purpose and Method for the Evaluation of Interpersonal Process in Health and Social Care', *Evaluation and Program Planning*, 31, pp. 34–40.

Holte-McKenzie, M., Forde, S. and Theobald, S. (2006) 'Development of a Participatory Monitoring and Evaluation Strategy', *Evaluation and Program Planning*, 29(4), pp. 365–376.

Horáková, N. (2005) Co je pro nas v zivote dulezite? ('What Is Important to Us in Our Lives?') *Journal Czech Society*, 2. Retrieved from https://cvvm.soc.cas.cz/media/com_form2content/documents/c7/a3692/f96/100045se_horakova-hodnoty%20EN.pdf.

Kluckhohn, C. (1951) Values and Value-Orientations in the Theory of Action. In Parsons, T. and Shils, E. (Eds.) *Toward a General Theory of Action*. Cambridge, MA: Harvard University Press, pp. 388–433.

Mottram, J. and Rust, C. (2008) 'The Pedestal and the Pendulum: Fine Art Practice, Research and Doctorates', *Journal of Visual Arts Practice*, 7(2), pp. 133–151.

Patton, Michael Quinn (2008) *Utilization-Focused Evaluation*. 4th edition. Thousand Oaks, CA: Sage Publications.

Peterson, J. C. (2010) 'CBPR in Indian Country: Tensions and Implications for Health Communication', *Health Communication*, 25(1), pp. 50–60.

Rokeach, M. (1973) *The Nature of Human Values*. New York: The Free Press.

Schlater, J. D. and Sontag, M. (1994) 'Towards the Measurement of Human Values', *Family and Consumer Science Research Journal*, 23(1), pp. 4–25.

Springett, J. (2003) Issues in Participatory Evaluation. In Wallerstein, M. N. (Ed.) *Community-based Participatory Research for Health*. San Francisco, CA: Jossey-Bass.

Steen, M., Manschot, M., and De Koning, N. (2011) 'Benefits of Co-design in Service Design Projects', *International Journal of Design*, 5(2), pp. 53–60.

van de Weijer, M., Van Cleempoel, K., and Heynen, H. (2014) 'Positioning Research and Design in Academia and Practice: A Contribution to a Continuing Debate', *Design Issues*, 30, pp. 17–29.

Visser, F. S., Stappers, P. J., van der Lugt , R., and Sanders E. B.-N. (2005) 'Context Mapping: Experiences from Practice', *CoDesign*, 1(2), pp. 119–149.

Wightman, F. (Fall 2010). Measures of Success: Not Everything that Counts Can Be Counted. *Vancouver Foundation Magazine*. Retrieved from http://vancouverfoundation. ca/documents/VanFdn-Magazine-Nov2010.pdf.

Zimmerman, J. and Forlizzi, J. (2008) 'The Role of Design Artifacts in Design Theory Construction', *Artifact*, 2(1), pp. 41–45.

2 Articulating values, designing processes

In this chapter, an early and basic values-based approach is described. We outline the development of an overall set of generalizable values statements about what is important to socially focused groups, and the associated indicators, as well as the design of the associated processes, based on participatory, dynamic and emergent mechanisms for generating and then validating shared values. It describes how a list of values statements and a design method were generated out of research through design and grounded theory approaches. It also demonstrates the iterative nature of the action research, as the research team continually learned from and alongside participating groups, so that – as the next chapter will show – many aspects of the value statements, participatory processes and assumed outcomes, were changed or modified.

The *Measuring Intangible Values* project started through a two-year collaborative project funded by the European Union Seventh Framework Program under a dedicated funding stream for 'Research for the Benefit of Specific Groups: Civil Society Organisations' (2009–2011). The funder's guidelines for this scheme specified that projects should be designed and implemented as partnerships between representatives of civil society organizations (CSOs) and academic researchers. Specifically, the scheme required the research questions to be developed primarily to meet real-world needs identified by the CSO partners, rather than emerging only from conversations within academic disciplines (ESDinds 2011).

The aim was to design values-based indicators and assessment tools that could be used to evaluate CSO projects in a manner considered valid to the CSO members, starting with a focus on those promoting Education for Sustainable Development (ESD) as interpreted in the widest sense possible. Quite soon the measurement of intangible, values-related outcomes emerged as a 'problem within a problem', – impossible to tackle from a single perspective because of its dissonance with established academic traditions and evaluation approaches. This meant that the whole team found themselves re-framing and co-designing the research project itself. From the start, then, there was recognition of the importance of being reflexive, and of building and respecting a multidisciplinary collaboration between academic and CSO partners. We further realized that in order for the project to be meaningful, we had to adopt an approach that valued and validated 'informal', non-academic and local ways of knowing – even if we thus had to reject narrow discipline-bound frameworks and tools. After an initial exploratory phase with a variety of prospective partners, a consortium was formed – called ESDinds – between two academic research institutions and four civil society organizations spread across diverse areas of interest and expertise.[1] The four CSO partners were chosen because they all acknowledged that they were struggling to articulate less tangible, values-related aspects of project impact, or to communicate them to donors and the public. The original motivation for a focus on intangible values was from our direct experience with these CSOs and their concerns that the most important aspect of their work – values, as in higher human values or ethics – was usually not appreciated by funders or wider society. The partners argued that if they could measure indicators related to what was 'important to them', which we interpreted as their values, that they could demonstrate many more 'soft' impacts of their work (Ebrahim 2002) and have more informed planning and ongoing evaluation. It was only as the ESDinds project developed that the central importance of this question to many, wider issues became apparent. This included soft indicators for societal wellbeing, moving 'beyond GDP measures' (e.g. Michaelson *et al.* 2009; Stiglitz, Sen, and Fitoussi 2009; Podger *et al.* 2012), missing aspects of sustainable development processes and evaluation (Burford *et al.* 2013), methods for reconceptualising effectiveness in environmental projects (Harder *et al.* 2014) and developing measures for the UN Sustainable Development Goals (Burford *et al.* 2016).

Values and their indicators

The initial work was to generate a new values-based approach, peer-elicited and co-developed with our CSO consortium partners, which was a complex piece of research in its own right. The process we undertook is shown diagrammatically in Figure 2.1. Rigorous empirical investigations with all four CSO consortium partners identified values or values-labels (such as 'respect') that were already in use, as well as specific indicators of these values (e.g. 'everyone feels they can offer their individual ideas to the group') as understood locally by each CSO. In addition, we tried to elicit any other ethical behaviours that they viewed as relevant to the 'success' of their projects. Data collection included semi-structured key informant interviews, questionnaires, field observations and documents analysis, with coding typology based on UNESCO guidelines (2007). This created a very large dataset, with a preliminary framework of 125 values, over 5,000 values statements, and 350 proto-indicators (that is, statements that capture the value in a concrete way, but not yet specific enough for localized use). Later chapters will show how initial assumptions about the relationships between these values and their indicators changed through time.

The first problem, though, was practical – the collaborative team found such a large number of values statements unwieldy and difficult to use. Through feedback and discussion, the initial statements were combined and prioritized down to five values and 177 proto-indicators. Consortium members selected subsets,

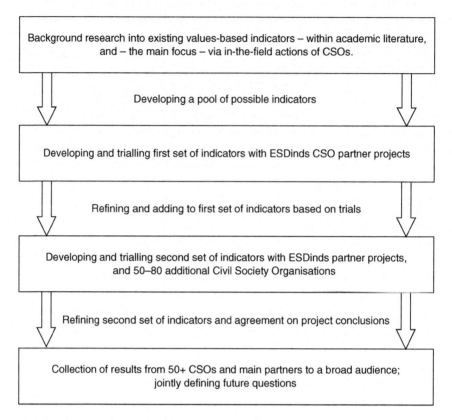

Background research into existing values-based indicators – within academic literature, and – the main focus – via in-the-field actions of CSOs.

Developing a pool of possible indicators

Developing and trialling first set of indicators with ESDinds CSO partner projects

Refining and adding to first set of indicators based on trials

Developing and trialling second set of indicators with ESDinds partner projects, and 50–80 additional Civil Society Organisations

Refining second set of indicators and agreement on project conclusions

Collection of results from 50+ CSOs and main partners to a broad audience; jointly defining future questions

Figure 2.1 Process diagram of developing values-based indicator and assessment tools within the very first, original project named ESDinds.

Source: adapted from Burford *et al.* (2015: 17) 'Making the Invisible Visible: Designing Values-Based Indicators and Tools for Identifying and Closing Values-Actions Gaps'.

focusing on clusters of values of high priority to them. An important point was that the researchers started the development of their values-based indicators in the field, not from theory alone. They visited several CSO groups and businesses beyond the core team, to listen, observe and question. From this analysis, 125 values were first identified. As the number of 125 was still far too many to use, these were clustered and grouped, and discussions took place across project partners to determine which 'clusters' were the most important to them. Five were chosen: Justice, Integrity, Unity in Diversity, Empowerment and Trust. The researchers then carried out literature reviews of these five values to determine how they were already viewed. With this in mind, they then returned to the collected data and drew out clusters of related concepts and indicators, using a grounded approach. The resulting 'themes' of 364 proto-indicators were presented to the partners for short listing. This was done on the basis of prioritised importance to these four CSOs. The CSOs were also asked to consider if there were gaps in the values/indicators of things that they thought were too important to miss out, and at this stage a sixth value was added: Care and Respect for the Community of Life. After appropriate development of indicators for this new value, the final list of six values with 177 Indicators was taken forward into field studies.

The finally agreed six values were Trust, Integrity, Empowerment, Justice, Unity in Diversity and Care and Respect for the Community of Life. Each of these values had approximately 20 associated indicators, except for the last, which had 79 as it was prepared with less time for careful culling. A sample of these values and indicators is given in Table 2.1, whilst the full list of these originally derived indicators is given in Appendix 1, at the back of this book.

Through our initial field trials it became clear that starting with the master list of indicators (as an enabling guide that could be edited, added to and modified) was more effective than starting from values words. At this point, we started to call these proto-indicators (that is, localizable prototypes, or templates, for generating measurable indicators). This was because it was the *indicators* that most helped individuals and groups clarify and make explicit what their underlying core values were (possibly because each was so concisely worded). Many other implications grew from this step, which will be explored later in the theme and case study sections. In the next chapter we also explain in detail how working with one particular CSO – Escheri – changed and improved our understanding of the most appropriate relationships between values and indicators, and how these became most relevant and effective to groups themselves.

Developing processes

As well as beginning to frame a set of shared values and associated indicators, the team was working together to design underpinning processes; both how the consortium operated, and how the values framework should be implemented with civil society organizations. As already outlined, from the start the aim was to have a project that was loosely structured, allowing for flexibility and responsiveness to partners' needs. The diversity of academic and professional backgrounds within the consortium already contributed to a multiplicity of understandings of key terms, such as 'values', 'evaluation', 'indicators' and 'Education for Sustainable Development (ESD)'. In addition, the design implicit in the consortium project process had included the creation of regular dedicated 'slots' for mutual learning and the construction of new, shared understandings within the project context: six monthly meetings where the CSOs were given the authority to decide on the next specific direction of research work. And by deciding early on to adopt a pragmatic and context-centred approach to validity, our conventional academic and discipline-based research methods needed to be creatively and continuously examined and transformed to be appropriate for the non-academic, informal learning context.

Table 2.1 Table showing arbitrarily chosen sample indicators as originally derived from clusters of those collected under each of the six values-words of the ESDinds project

Value-label	Initial Indicators
Empowerment	People feel they are encouraged to reach their potential
	People have a sense of power that they can effect change
	Everyone knows what their responsibility is within the organization, and feels responsibility for their part of the work
	People feel that they are encouraged to express their opinion
	Mistakes are understood as opportunities to learn and improve
Integrity	People's behaviour is consistent with their words
	Financial integrity is measured and communicated internally or externally
	Resource use efficiency is measured and communicated internally or externally
	Goals are reviewed between committed parties to determine what has and has not been achieved
	Truth-seeking, non-judgmental, confidential channels are in place for individuals/teams seeking guidance on the application of ethics, reporting violations and examining violations of ethics
Justice	People feel they have an equal opportunity to voice their opinions
	People feel that their opinions are respected
	Decision-making processes provide for equal representation
	The organization acts in a manner that is impartial and non-discriminatory (not discriminating on the basis of race, colour, sex, sexual orientation, creed, religion, national or ethnic origin)
	People participate actively in making decisions about issues that affect their lives
Respect and Care for the Community of Life	Work environment is supportive of people being able to act with care in their families or personal relationships
	People feel that their own individual identity and approach is respected
	The organization respects and acknowledges the contributions of others to its work, and gives credit for the outcomes to those who contributed
	The environment/community of life is celebrated
	The organization acts to reduce its environmental impact or remedy its contribution to environmental problems
Trust	Partners are trusted to follow through on their commitments without the need for formal agreements
	Entity is transparent about the outcomes of decision-making
	People are perceived to be transparent
	People are perceived to be truthful
	Trusted partners are given flexibility to do things differently within a prescribed structure
Unity in Diversity	Teams include members with different characteristics (e.g. gender, culture, age and other aspects of individual difference such as personality)
	Learning processes accommodate different learning styles
	People share their skills and abilities freely with one another, regardless of nationality, ethnic origin, skin colour, gender, sexual orientation, creed or religion
	People are inclusive (talk to everyone and no one is left out)
	People feel that they create something better or greater as a group than on their own

Source: originally printed in Podger *et al.* (2013) 'Can Values Be Measured? Significant Contributions from a Small Civil Society Organization Through Action Research', *Action Research*, 11(1), pp. 11–12.

Note
These are arbitrarily chosen examples, selected by the authors from a much longer list (over 100 Indicators in total). The assignation of these Indicators to these or other value-labels may be subjective or inter-subjective. The use of values-words was later dropped, as the direct use of the indicators was found much more effective.

As the consortium project developed, so did its frameworks for interaction with specific civil society organizations. We aimed to define this process as a sequence of outline steps. These were always an oversimplification, with the boundaries between steps often blurred – in some individual case study projects more than others – and there were usually several different ways of achieving each step. Steps could be difficult to articulate while they were evolving, and each one took time to clarify and understand. Our focus was on achieving the agreed brief for the consortium project – workable, locally valid measures of values-based achievements. Within the context of a time-limited, multiple-partner initiative, everything else in the path seemed less important: we were eager to work with our CSO practitioner co-researchers to achieve a set of methods, and then a toolbox, which was appropriate for them. This was our guiding and driving principle: to achieve pragmatic and valid co-developed tools of use to the local practitioners. This goal was fully met in three out of four of the partner CSOs. In the fourth organization, significant steps forward were taken in the last few weeks of the project, although many challenges remained; issues which will be addressed later.

However, as we grappled with designing a coherent and generalizable sequence of steps within the complex process of co-designing, prototyping and testing (proto) indicators and assessment tools, we encountered many theoretical and practical challenges, and additional research questions were generated. As Figure 2.2 shows, the conventional view of relationships between values, indicators and their assessment is schematically straightforward, assuming limited overlaps between values, and a non-iterative process.

When we looked for a more open-ended and iterative approach, we found many research conversations about this in different disciplines, including psychology, evaluation, environmental management, environmental indicators,

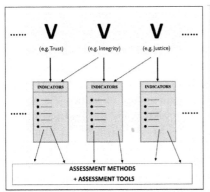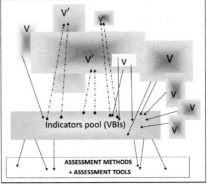

Figure 2.2 Comparative schematic representations of how values are structured (1) according to traditional academic notions and (2) as reported in the field by one group of NGO co-researchers.

Source: adapted from Podger *et al.* (2013: 13).

education, and even health studies. By starting from a research through design method we aimed instead to follow the key questions over a period of time, engaging with open conversations within each discipline through the literature, and ultimately looking – as RtD aims to do – to construct a platform of new knowledge that could transcend disciplinary boundaries and assumptions. Figure 2.2 thus also shows the schematic differences to a more conventional approach, to illustrate how we conceptualized our alternative process. In this more fuzzy model, the lack of linear borders represents the subjective/inter-subjective (i.e. non-objective) definition of values and indicators. Different combinations of indicators derived from values, V, from given persons can be localized by other persons and used to represent new locally inter-subjective values, V'. These values can have a variety of relationships to each other, including containing and overlapping. And crucially, proto-indicators are both pooled (rather than being articulated as a 'tree' of separate statements) and form the basis from which values are generated and agreed. It should be noted that this diagram visualizes the way the consortium project itself developed its thinking through time, with some of these aspects not fully realized (such as the pooling of indicators) until several stages through the field trial testing. These changes, and their implications, will be drawn out throughout the rest of this book.

In working towards the project goal of designing values-based indicators, we also realised that these could not be validated in an abstract way, through theoretical work or by setting up artificial 'experiments' in the style of existing schools of study of values. Rather, the only way to understand the comprehensibility, relevance, measurability and usefulness (or otherwise) of the prototype indicators was by testing them in real CSO evaluation contexts, a process that will be described in much greater detail in the next chapter, through working with Echeri Consultores, a non-profit organization based in Michoacan, Mexico.

Developing a 'toolkit'

The original toolkit for the values-based approach was designed to be an effective conceptual method for linking external, observable conditions with personal or organizational values, in order to achieve rigorous individual (subjective) and collective (inter-subjective) measurements of values. As already noted, the partner-developed version of the toolkit ready for field testing initially consisted of a reference set of 177 values-based indicators, to which was added guidance on their application. The next stage of the ESDinds research project was therefore to investigate whether the proposed toolkit could be applied by real CSOs, in a manner that was useful and meaningful to CSO stakeholders. A core requirement of this phase was that any assessment methods developed for the indicators had to be feasible within the respective CSO contexts. Several preliminary field studies were carried out for this purpose, in a very diverse sample of organisations and environments. These showed that some indicators needed adapting, giving a final set of 166. Some also caused shifts in understanding, prompting changes in the processes used in applying the proto-type toolkit. This will be explored in much greater depth in the next chapter. In subsequent field studies, however, no further changes of process were necessary, and it was possible to evaluate the feasibility and usefulness of a 'complete' toolkit – which we called 'WeValue' – with a range of different organisations (Burford *et al.* 2012).

In this next version of the toolkit design, the list of 166 proto-indicators were presented in a 'menu' format in a workshop, where they helped user CSOs to identify and crystallise what intangible values were important to them, and those they wished to evaluate (Table 2.2). Through a shared process of discussing and selecting from this indicator list, participants could make explicit their own perspectives, and then start group discussions to negotiate what their shared values might be. By keeping in mind they ultimately wished to have concise statements lending themselves to being measured, participants negotiated words and the meanings in them until they reached an overall consensus. In this process the group members also could begin to see where they might have goals not yet met – where there are gaps – and where there are big differences between their goals and where their activities might actually lead them.

Thus, the proto-indicators as provided were personalized and localized into true indicators which could be measured. This could be by changing words to reflect their own understandings more precisely, or by enabling the perspectives of different participants (staff, volunteers, management, etc.,) to be explicitly and clearly articulated.

Next we had to decide who participates in the CSO values and evaluation process. When using the values-based toolkit in these early studies, the user CSOs determined the type and level of internal participation in the process. For example, some involved only lead staff, others all levels of the CSO personnel and some even included wider stakeholders from society. Sometimes only the leaders carried out measurements of the indicators, in others the entire process was collective. Examples given in an early version of the 'WeValue Handbook' included:

1   The leaders/management choose the indicators and measurement methods, design assessment tools, collect data, analyse the results and report back to the community.
2   As above, but the wider project community provides advice and input, especially in the design.
3   There is equal involvement of leaders and project community members throughout.
4   The management hands over to the staff, volunteers and/or project beneficiaries to make all the decisions, design of assessment methods and reports.

The development of the values-based framework toolkit was evolved to ensure groups had the flexibility to choose levels and types of participation that worked

Table 2.2 Sample indicator shortlist from WeValue toolkit (2013: 16)

Indicator	1 Very important	2 Important	3 Slightly important	4 Not important	Taken for granted?	Useful to measure?
Everyone has their place in the team						
Work environment is supportive of people being able to fulfil their responsibilities in their families or personal relationships						
Decision-making takes into account the social, economic and environmental needs of future generations						
People participate actively in developing the group's code of ethics						
Women feel that they are given equal opportunities to participate in decision-making processes						
People share their skills and abilities freely with one another, regardless of nationality, ethnic origin, skin colour, gender, sexual orientation, creed or religion						
People are taking the opportunity to develop their own visions and goals for projects, and/or for the whole group						
Group's activities or events connect participants emotionally to the community of life						
Mistakes are understood as opportunities to learn and improve						
People do not back-bite about others within the group						
People feel that they can participate in the vision and activities of the group or project without compromising their personal beliefs or values						
Actions of individuals are consistent and in harmony with the core principles promoted by the group						
People invest their own time and resources in activities that benefit the environment or society						
People have a sense of power that they can effect change						

Truth-seeking, non-judgmental, confidential channels are in place for individuals/teams seeking guidance on the application of ethics, reporting violations and examining violations of ethics

Financial integrity is communicated internally or externally

Action is consciously taken to contribute to a greater respect for nature

The environment and community of life is celebrated

Group acts to protect the environment, without waiting for governments or others to act first

Group implements a policy of sustainable waste management, e.g. recycling or reducing waste

Source: available for free download from: http://blogs.brighton.ac.uk/wevalue/files/2016/03/WE-VALUE-shorter-toolkit_2015-1aam0zp.pdf.

best for them, based on the structure of the organization as well as pragmatic issues of time and resources. From the CSO's perspective, maintaining fitness for purpose may require the active and meaningful participation of senior staff members at the earliest stages of the evaluation, namely co-inception and co-design. However, this does not mean that consensus needs to be achieved for every single participant in the measuring part of the values-based evaluation. For that, the key group is the evaluator group, those who will carry out the analysis and use the results. If large and inclusive, the inter-subjective validity of the results would be improved. In a less participatory group, or a group where the participants will be mostly young children, for example, the interpretive process (of what the indicators would look like operationalized in the work of the CSO) may be concentrated in a smaller number of people, for example, the project managers.

This flexible approach is an example of our balancing of scientific rigour and validity against convenience and usability, which was constantly embedded in the toolkit design. The purpose of the measures we wished to have as outputs of the CSO using the toolkit, were to enable the CSO to judge their success with respect to their intrinsic social values, and be able to communicate these to their funders and the public. It is thus the CSOs who must create the inter-subjective understanding of 'fitness for purpose' within their own specific context. Clearly, much will depend on the exact purposes to which they put their measures. It might be no more than a monitoring exercise or formative evaluation, intended to help the CSO concerned to understand its strengths and weaknesses and to improve its activities in an evidence-based way; or it might be a summative evaluation to a large donor, with jobs or even the future of the organizations at stake. The final section of this book will illustrate how some of these different goals were achieved, whilst the conclusion will review the importance of different kinds of 'evaluation influence'.

The last element to consider in this initial phase was assessment – how to make measurements that CSOs could use for effective self-evaluation, based on indicators that were valid for the group itself. In order to be able to link value indicators to measurement, a second 'menu' or library of methods was developed and provided for CSOs to consider, accompanied by guidance notes. This was to introduce to the CSO users some differences in evaluating beliefs and feelings compared to what people actually do, as well as the constraints/benefits of using different methods. Participants were asked to think about what each indicator meant in their own specific context, and to consider how they could gather evidence that would enable them to judge how effectively they were achieving that value indicator. This naturally also involves thinking about potentially using a range of methods to obtain measures. For cases where stronger representation of an indicator was needed, methods to obtain different and triangulating measures were suggested. The methods outlined in Table 2.3 are fairly typical approaches from the social sciences; as we will show later, working with CSOs led to these being expanded and extended, particularly as visual and verbal as well as written modes of data gathering.

Table 2.3 Extract from a 'menu' of assessment methods presented to participants during field visits trialling the first two sets of indicators

Method	Description
Survey	Gathering of information through a form containing a set of questions, especially one addressed to a statistically significant number of subjects considered to be representative of a whole.
Interview	A conversation with an individual in which the researcher asks questions in a systematic way. Can be structured (a specific set of questions asked in the same words and in the same order), semi-structured (a specific set of questions that are used as prompts for a broader discussion), and unstructured (a discussion with no pre-planned questions or order, naturally emerging from the conversation).
Focus group	A discussion by a small group of people (typically 6 to 12 individuals) of selected topics of interest in informal or formal settings. The focus group discussion is typically directed by a facilitator who guides the discussion in order to obtain the group's opinions about or reactions to specific themes or issues.
Observation	The systematic observation of an interaction, process, community or group. This can be done through observation alone or by both observing and participating (participant observation), to varying degrees, in the group's daily activities. Observers make careful notes about what they see, recording all accounts and observations as field notes in a field notebook. This can be structured (looking out for and/or rating a specific list of items), semi-structured (looking out for a broad set of themes) or unstructured (deriving any categories or questions from the observation itself), and can be carried out by individuals or by groups.
Document analysis	The systematic search for information, evidence or insight about a research question in documents directly or indirectly related to, and/or produced by, the research subjects.
Indirect measures	The systematic gathering of information in a way that does not interact directly with the participants.
Forum theatre	In this process the actors or audience members could stop a performance, often a short scene in which a character was being oppressed in some way. The audience would suggest different actions for the actors to carry out on-stage in an attempt to change the outcome of what they were seeing.

Source: reprinted from Burford *et al.* (2013) 'Field Trials of a Novel Toolkit for Evaluating "Intangible" Vales-Related Dimensions of Projects', *Evaluation and Program Planning*, 36, p. 4.

The values-based toolkit thus had three separate elements to be evaluated for their usefulness, meaningfulness and relevance in the field: the selected value proto-indicators, the potential of methods for measuring localized indicators, and the effectiveness of the overall participatory process. This was both about the effectiveness as perceived by different organisations, and the overall usefulness of the entire toolkit to a wider sample of CSOs beyond the initial partners.

Whilst field trials were later held with several groups, we will focus in the next chapter on the experience of early working with one particular organization, because of how particularly powerful this was in co-developing the project as a whole.

Note

1 The consortium was comprised of two research institutions (University of Brighton, UK, and Charles University Environment Center, Prague, Czech Republic) and four civil society organizations (Alliance of Religions and Conservation, Earth Charter Initiative, European Baha'i Business Forum and People's Theater).

References

Burford, G., Valasco, I., Janoušková, S., Zahradnik, M., Hak, T., Podger, D., Piggot, G., and Harder, M. K. (2012) 'Field Trials of a Novel Toolkit for Evaluating "Intangible" Values-Related Dimensions of Projects', *Evaluation and Program Planning*, 36(1), pp. 1–14.

Burford, G., Hoover, E., Velasco, I., Janoušková, S., Jimenez, A., Piggot, G., Podger, D., and Harder, M. K. (2013) 'Bringing the "Missing Pillar" into Sustainable Development Goals: Towards Intersubjective Values-Based Indicators', *Sustainability*, 5(7), pp. 3035–3059.

Burford, G., Tamás, P., and Harder, M. K. (2016) 'Can We Improve Indicator Design for Complex Sustainable Development Goals? A Comparison of a Values-Based and Conventional Approach', *Sustainability*, 8(9), 861.

Ebrahim, A. (2002) 'Information Struggles: The Role of Information in the Reproduction of NGO-funder Relationships', *Nonprofit and Voluntary Sector Quarterly*, 31(1), pp. 84–114.

ESDinds, (2011) *ESDinds: The development of values-based indicators and assessment tools for civil society organizations promoting education for sustainable development. Deliverable 17: Final project report to European Commission Seventh Framework Programme* (FP7/2007–2013), www.esdinds.eu, University of Brighton.

Harder, Marie K., Velasco, I., Burford, G., Podger, D., Janoušková, S., Piggot, G., and Hoover, E. (2014) 'Reconceptualizing "Effectiveness" in Environmental Projects: Can We Measure Values-related Achievements?' *Journal of Environmental Management*, 139, pp. 120–134.

Michaelson, J., Abdallah, S., Steuer, N., Thompson, S., and Marks, N. (2009). *National Accounts of Well-Being: Bringing Real Wealth onto the Balance Sheet*. London: The New Economics Foundation.

Podger, D., Velasco, I., Amezcua Luna, C., Burford, G., and Harder, M. K. (2012) 'Can Values Be Measured? Significant Contributions from a Small Civil Society Organisation Through Action Research', *Action Research*, 11(1), pp. 8–30.

Stiglitz, J. E., Sen, A., and Fitoussi, J.-P. (2009). *Report by the Commission on the Measurement of Economic Performance and Social Progress*. OFCE Retrieved from: www.ofce.sciences-po.fr/pdf/dtravail/WP2009-33.pdf.

UNESCO (2007). *Asia-Pacific Guidelines for the Development of National ESD Indicators*. Bangkok: UNESCO Asia and Pacific Regional Bureau for Education.

3 Developing a values-based approach
The case of Echeri

As the last chapter concluded, the next step in developing a values-based toolkit and associated participation process was testing the prototype through application in real-world contexts. We wanted to find out if the values and proto-indicators developed in the first stage were relevant or useful for civil society organizations. We wanted to see if they could be implemented practically and effectively by such groups, and whether they could be used to generate associated measures for self-evaluation that were both appropriate and valid. One of these projects was Echeri Consultores, a non-profit organization that works with children and youth, with the aim of reconnecting them to their local environment. The research team initially thought they would be focusing on what constituted valid measures for this group, as well as appropriate assessment methods of those measures. In keeping with our attitude of co-production of knowledge, this next stage could only be undertaken as a participatory and co-designing process, and since the CSO was unlikely to have experience of evaluation concepts, the variety of methods, or how to make sure that selected measures were valid, these concepts had to be explored together. For example, could a questionnaire be valid to measure 'equal voice'? What type? Academics and practitioners would have to work together very closely: they would have to educate each other and listen to each other through open dialogue and reciprocity. This was not a research activity that could be pre-planned in detail, but one that would require the researchers to learn iteratively from each other, modify their worldviews, re-examine any implications in the working context of the CSO and modify their research directions until they arrived at a new, shared understanding that was useful.

The main research question intended at this stage, then, was what assessment methods could be found (such as surveys and structured observations) with specific assessment tools (e.g. a survey having children run to different spots for different answers) that were appropriate in the field to measure the indicators associated with a CSO chosen value. If so, the link between the measures and the indicators would be partially validated. Fuller validation of the framework would require more work: for example, different types of measurements from different perspectives for a given indicator, and several indicators for a given value (ESDinds, 2011). Our crucial principle for validity, already mentioned, required that Echeri 'recognize' itself in terms of the results, that is, that the values and their measurements were meaningful to the group conducting the evaluation – an issue that is often neglected in traditional values measurements. This will be returned to in detail in Chapter 6, where we explore values and their validity in much greater depth.

Whilst working with Echeri did enable values and indicators to be selected and modified effectively for their own situation, the most important aspect of this project turned out to be a much deeper learning – in fact it reshaped some core research questions. This is because of the necessary pre-task for the joint team to explicitly understand Echeri's unarticulated shared values: to draw tacit feelings, knowledge and thoughts into crystallized statements. In this chapter we describe what happened and the effect on the overall research design and practice, before going on in the following chapters to show how our unexpected findings fed back into our development work, and our interaction with future groups.

Testing the use of values and proto-indicators

Echeri Consultores is a non-profit civil society organization based in Michoacan, Mexico, affiliated with one of the original EU project partners, the Earth Initiative. They focus on using values education, based on the Earth Charter, to help children and youth reconnect with their locality, particularly around environment reforestation and ecological awareness. Testing the values-indicator toolkit took place across two strands of Echeri's core activities. The first involved working with 15 schools in Purepecha indigenous communities that aimed to give children the knowledge, attitudes and skills to serve as custodians of their local environment. Using arts, dance and other participatory methodologies, the founding director organized in each school a sequence of workshops with 40–60 children, beginning with general awareness of environmental conservation and connecting the children to the values of care and respect for the community of life. These were followed by guided reflection on their own local ecosystem, technical workshops leading to the creation of tree nurseries tended by the children themselves, and finally reforestation in school grounds and local communities.

The second Echeri programme consisted of a multicultural group of 19 youth called Juatarhu ('Forest' in Purepecha), spanning in age from 12 to 21 and including indigenous and non-indigenous, urban and rural, locally born and immigrant youth, that had been meeting weekly for one year. The Juatarhu group focuses on education for sustainable development, again using the arts as a core medium. For example, they organize large reforestation campaigns and municipality-wide arts festivals, as well as working on projects linked with other groups nationwide. When the founding director of Echeri was originally asked to collaborate with the research project, she expressed scepticism that actual measurable indicators could ever be derived for the intangible values that underpinned her group's activities. However, the six values othat had already been derived by the EU project – empowerment, justice, integrity, trustworthiness, unity in diversity and care and respect for the community of life – resonated strongly with Echeri's own mission, which created an interest in going further.

Generating a shared understanding of the concept of measurement as it relates to values presented the first major challenge. The director's starting point was the assumption that external researchers would be likely to assess the organization against an externally derived numerical scale and judge Echeri to have, for example, '50% love'. Through discussion it was agreed that the suggested indicators could be thought of as 'making the invisible visible', and could provide Echeri with a vocabulary to articulate its impact more explicitly to its funder in terms of core values, according to its own internal criteria. On this basis, Echeri agreed to participate in the co-research process.

At this stage all the values proto-indicators were organized, as separated lists, under the six value headings. Participants were asked to choose from these values headings first, and then select the relevant associated indicators. With the Juatarhu youth, this was done as equal partners through a workshop, talking about what the values meant to them. As Cardiela Amezcua-Luna, the Echeri Consultores founder and director put it:

> Very beautiful things happened during that workshop. We spent two hours discussing what the values meant and how they related to each other, and in the end we decided that we want to focus on two values – Collaboration in Diversity and Care and Respect for the Community of Life – because these are at the heart of everything we do. For us, respect is the basis for all other values; love arises from respect, and integrity from love and so on. But diversity is also very important to us because our project encompasses different ages, different communities, some of them indigenous, some in transition from rural to urban settings.
>
> (WeValue 2015: 3)

Agreeing and measuring indicators localized from the proto-indicators

The next step was to agree indicators for these selected values, starting with the proto-indicators for each value. In the process of translating statements accurately into Spanish, Amezcua-Luna also found that they were exploring how to express these better, to more properly fit their specific project. An additional aspect of using a large list of proto-indicators was that it suggested explicit consideration of some practices that were happening but that had not previously articulated. For example, when an indicator thought to be unimportant was used, and the youth were asked if, 'Women/girls feel that they are valued, and have equal access to information and decision-making' Amezcua-Luna noticed that all immediately indicated, without thinking about it, 'A lot':

> There was no hesitation. It was a question they'd never asked themselves, because it was always there. But in a country, in a region full of sexism, where women do not have that access generally, the youth realised that the project has generated a space of equity. As a project team, and myself as

director, we had generated this space consciously, but at that moment the youth really became aware of it.

(WeValue 2015: 4–5)

The process similarly enabled the youth to understand one another better and to value much more what they were doing, e.g. for Collaboration in Diversity: 'They've always felt very united, but now they know why they're united' (ibid.: 5). The group also worked collaboratively on choosing assessment techniques. Whilst the researcher initially suggested a survey, the group wanted to act in a more participatory and non-verbal way. Amexcua-Luna's idea was to use a large spiral shape, made of cloths laid out on the ground:

> That's a symbol used ancestrally over time by indigenous communities in Mexico, and at Echeri we include it in most of our exercises. So my idea was to make a big spiral on the ground out of different coloured scarves, and have each colour mean a different answer. When we asked the survey question, the youth had to go and stand on the colour that best represented their answer to the question. This method was really valuable because we could assess how the group as a whole was doing, and at the same time, how each individual was positioned within the group.

(Ibid.: 4)

An example shows the way in which this assessment process not only gave a picture of how participants thought the group was doing in relation to its chosen value indicators, but also had transformative effects on agreed behaviours. In relation to an original indicator – 'group norms exist and they are followed' – the young people were asked 'Do you respect the norms that Juatarhu has set?' Their response might be said to be lukewarm; everyone went to the part of the spiral that said 'more or less' (Figure 3.1). This, in turn, enabled beliefs about, and attitudes to, informal norms to be explicitly articulated and debated; and led to agreement that norms (such as arriving on time and keeping the blog updated) should indeed be met, without the requirement for formal pressure or rules – an agreement that was taken up by everyone, following the workshop.

Ultimately then, a values-based system that combines open-endedness with rigorous appraisal offered Echeri a new way forward for enabling and judging their success:

DIRECTOR: Before [the project] my only evaluation method was collective reflection about past action. We would reflect on the objectives, context, resources, results, foreseen and unforeseen obstacles, impact, and proposals for follow-up … how could I measure? I could see values there in the relationships and the commitment, but I couldn't see how it was possible to measure. Through dialogue, we were gradually arriving at the complexities and translating it into something marvellously simple that gave deep information.

(Podger *et al.* 2013: 25)

Figure 3.1 Illustration of a localized measurement for a local indicator: spatial survey. The children run to the point on the spiral that represents the strength of their answer to a question such as, 'Do girls have as much respect as boys in our group?' A photograph of their positions becomes the measure in this case.

Source: photograph provided with permission, by Cardiela Amezcua Luna.

In particular, these measures were valid to the CSO, linking actions on the ground to their underlying values: 'It was validating the overall method, beyond the concrete results of the action. It allowed me to measure the human results, more than the action results' (ibid.: 25).

With conventional research methods it would have been enough to elicit an objective, positivistic response and simply report that all six values headings were considered relevant – a partial confirmation of our prototype toolkit – and that two were considered sufficiently important to warrant immediate trials of their proto-indicators. However, by using a research through design approach, much richer and more useful results were obtained that both enhanced the outcomes for the case study group, and could be fed in to and used to modify the ongoing research. This was first about variations in the 'structural' importance of core values to different organisations. From the original core six values, it became clear that – for Echeri – some were understood as being central and generative, and that others were perceived as effects or results: they did not have the kind of equal status usually portrayed in academic literature. What's more, what was contained within a value concept such as Trust or Integrity could vary across individuals and within groups, showing that these are not fixed or objective. Second was the crucial importance of local context and the specificity of each group's engagement with its own particular intangible value system. These issues are next explored in turn.

Variations in the structural importance of values

Even before arranging discussions with the youth, the Echeri Director, Amezcua-Luna, had removed two of the six values because she viewed them as 'non-structural': trust and empowerment. She explained later to the academics that she considered both of these instead as 'outcomes/results/effects':

DIRECTOR: Trust is a result of everything else that we do. Trust comes after they get to know you. They know that you have the other values and that generates trust.

RESEARCHER: What about empowerment?

DIRECTOR: Empowerment is also a result. In Echeri's projects, empowerment is not a goal in itself but the result of a process. Youth can not only demand their rights, but exercise their rights.

> Through further dialogue [the director] emphasized that trust and empowerment were general, indirect outcome values that would be difficult to target as specific, focused goals to achieve as ends in themselves; therefore, they were not priorities for measurement.

(Podger *et al.* 2013: 16)

These discussions suggested that – unlike in most values measurement literature – values were not necessarily ranked and rated on an equal footing. Some could be seen as structurally central, underpinning principles, whilst others were better understood as outcomes. This showed that the prototype values-indicator toolkit needed amendment, since an 'end-effect' or outcome value was likely to span many other core values. Most crucially, it was important *not* to make a direct correlation between particular values and specific indicators. As illustrated in the previous chapter, rather than a tree-like hierarchy of values to indicators, there is in fact a much more overlapping matrix of relationships, which we increasingly understood as a 'pool' of indicators.

It also became clear that the original naming of core values was problematic when applied to a specific situation. The selected four values defined as core by Echeri – Justice, Integrity, Unity in Diversity and Care and Respect for the Community of Life – were submitted to a deeper critical dialogue in the youth focus group, where the youth were given full control over decision-making. (The affiliated indicators were not introduced at this stage in this particular field trial.) The youth documented their definitions and real-life examples for each value. The Director then returned and facilitated the identification of relationships between each pair of values. The youth were not comfortable with the term 'Unity in Diversity' because they felt it implied some uniformity, but when the researcher outlined its general intended meaning it was then felt to be meaningful and relevant, and renamed 'Collaboration in Diversity'.

The youth also understood 'Integrity' in terms of ecological integrity, without the researchers' intended further dimensions of moral integrity, with aspects of moral conduct, authenticity, consistency and the application of ethical values.

These points make the research team increasingly aware of the complexity of interpretation of values headings across cultural and geo-political domains, regardless of the care taken in the original definition phase to avoid such problems, and the expert translation skills present in the field. Again, this was contrary to mainstream academic values measurement reports, where 'concept-naming' powers tend to remain with the evaluators. In fact, it was the modifications and rephrasings such as 'Collaboration in Diversity' – where initial values become completely localized to the specific organization – that led to real ownership and a sense of genuine connection to the values concept under discussion (Table 3.1).

Initially, the university researchers were concerned, because such significant differences in interpretation could mean that the values were not generalizable, for example, to other organizations, and, because of that, the related 'downstream' indicators and assessment methods could never be valid or more widely

Table 3.1 Original and modified versions of indicators for 'Care and Respect for the Community of Life' developed through participation with a small environmental NGO, Echeri Consultores, Mexico

---

Indicators

Partners, member organizations and individuals do not feel that they have compromised their beliefs by participating in the vision and activities of the organization/project

MODIFIED TO:

Members and societies feel that they can maintain their beliefs while participating in the vision and activities of Juatarhu

Different points of view are heard and incorporated

Degree to which members/partners feel that their individual identity and approach has been respected

People are encouraged to reach their potential

Everyone has his/her place in the team

Learning processes accommodate different learning styles

Individuals have a feeling of a unified work environment

Individuals learn together, share skills, abilities and information freely with one another regardless of creed, colour, ethnicity, gender

Members are inclusive (talk to everyone and no one is left out)

Group norms exist. People follow the group norms

Women believe they are valued

MODIFIED TO:

Women believe they are valued, and have equal access to information and decision-making

People feel they create something better/greater as a group than on their own

---

applicable. However, as already outlined in Chapter 1, the project's guiding principle was that the final values-indicator framework that we wished to develop needed to be considered valid by the CSOs themselves. This is known as unitary validity. The existing prototype toolkit and its underlying development approach needed to be open-ended and open-minded enough to enable local modification; in fact, it should be designed to *facilitate* local interpretations and localizations. By observing what transpired, we could learn lessons from Echeri about how to create both value concepts and their development process. The extent to which Collaboration in Diversity was a 'new' value as opposed to a variation of the original Unity in Diversity would simply have to unfold, as would any other implications.

The critical examination by the youth focus group also provided more opportunities for mutual learning about how they understood relationships between values. The following exchange is from a post-workshop unstructured key informant interview:

RESEARCHER: How did you select the values that you wanted to measure?
DIRECTOR: All of them seemed important but we prioritized them.... We were considering respect as structural and equity as a result of respect.
RESEARCHER: What do you mean when you say that respect was structural?
DIRECTOR: Respect is a basic premise in our methodology; it is structural as in fundamental. Respect is the basis of the spiral. I respect myself, my companions, my community, in opening the spiral I am widening the scope. Respect as a basis and a guide generates the other values.... The result of respect is love, then integrity, equity, collaboration, solidarity.

(Podger *et al.* 2013: 17)

Through further dialogue it emerged that Respect was seen as a cornerstone, on which other values could be built. The spiral represented to the Echeri youth the integration of human beings to the environment – a non-anthropocentric vision of belonging. The concept of 'bringing youth into the spiral' refers to helping them understand their true selves and acknowledge one another. The spiral symbol is also used to represent actions that are initiated at a very local level (e.g. friends) and grows towards a global vision. This context explains why the group chose to represent their values as a spiral, with Respect at the centre. Collaboration in Diversity was seen as a specific value present only when all the other five values were present, and thus also useful to measure.

The level of shared understanding and consensual detail that the Echeri participants developed in their workshop about overall relationships between the different values was unexpected for the researchers. It emphasized that there were different perceptions of even the six values that had been originally agreed by the consortium project group; different ways of articulating their meanings, overlaps and relative structural roles; but also the possibility of considerable agreement across a group's participants. The possibility of developing a useful repeatable framework for values measurement with any generalizability seemed, at this point, to be fading away. At the same time, it was clear that the demo-cratic, collaborative process used in critical inquiry, meaning-making and examination of practice enabled the youth and the founding director to contex-tualize our values-based indicators to their local situation and make it work for them. It helped them to develop a shared understanding and emancipatory knowledge (Kemmis 2001) that they could then make use of to develop their own uniquely localised indicators and assessment tools.

Specifically, critical and deep considerations of values and practices, and sub-sequent empowerment of all involved in the research (Lather 1986) led to transformational learning, with the youth going on to crystallize their under-standing of Respect as the most fundamental value, and Collaboration in Diver-sity as an all-encompassing one. As reflected in the following statement made by a Juatarhu youth, the group were enabled to deepen awareness of the self and make their beliefs and understandings visible, opening the possibilities for social action and choice (Lather 1986):

> With this experience we became aware that values are present without us even mentioning them, because they are an essential part of our sharing and our view of the world, and when they become visible we feel more united and strengthened, more closely reflected in and identified with the Earth Charter. Somehow, we became more conscious of who we are and what we do; we valued and understood ourselves more.
>
> ('Eduardo', field note made by researcher, 24 April 2010,
> quoted in Podger *et al.* 2013: 18)

This learning was therefore clearly rich and transformational; something we needed to investigate further. This was both about what was happening to the group undertaking the evaluation, and beyond it to the consortium project overall. This is because, in terms of the values-based toolkit design develop-ment, we were discovering key relational factors that both differed from many conventional evaluation paradigms, and that needed to be tested and applied in different contexts, to explore generalizability beyond this particular field trial. To summarize, these findings were that:

- Value sub-concepts that define a value domain are more important that the terms or phrases used;
- It was not useful to tie each proto-indicator to only one value;
- Proto-indicators were more 'universal' than the value headings for which they had been derived;
- Proto-indicators were not considered valid by the user CSO without being 'localized' to their specific circumstances.

We have already underlined the crucial importance of local context and the specificity of each group's engagement to the framing of its own intangible value concepts. The next question was therefore to explore the implications of this for deciding on measurement indicators and methods.

Participation, localization and evaluation

In the second step of the field-testing, Echeri explored the relevance of the indicators associated with the two values they had prioritized – Respect and Collaboration in Diversity – and selected the ones they wished to measure. The research team had originally envisioned a stepwise process for this, as follows:

a   indicators for the chosen values headings would be translated into Spanish;
b   a list of over 30 sample assessment methods, prepared in advance by the researchers, would also be translated;
c   a few methods would be selected;
d   specific assessment tools, appropriate for that CSO would be developed;
e   data would be collected and analysed.

During the field visit, however, we soon realized that what was required was not a verbatim translation that treated the indicators and the methods list as rigid, predefined research instruments. Rather, Escheri needed to create meanings for them that would be relevant in their own context, and that would combine validity with practical utility. What transpired was thus an integrated process in which the translation and localization (customization) of the indicators was underpinned by discussions about how they might be measured. This began with the Director being given the list of all 79 indicators for Respect and Care for the Community of Life and prioritizing them in order. The group then met to first discuss what kind of assessment methodologies seemed most appropriate – that is, about what they wanted to measure and how. It was only after this process that the group talked about the individual indicators.

Amezcua-Luna was asked to identify which indicators were important, unrelated to how these could be measured. She reported that all 12 for Unity in Diversity as well as ten out of 79 for Respect and Care were significantly relevant:

> We saw that some of the indicators fitted like a ring to the finger. They were the ones about education for sustainability, environmental action, contribution to the respect of nature and especially eco-systemic understanding. This is the focus of our project, this is a core aspect.
> (Interview notes, 6 June 2010, quoted in Podger *et al.* 2013: 19)

This was, again, a process of localizing the indicators to the particular context – of making the indicators specifically meaningful to this organization and its goals. In fact, it was through this process of localization that members were able to come to a consensus about their meaning and appropriateness. Although this need for localization was anticipated (to some degree) by the research team, its importance as a necessary step in making the entire process both relevant and valid to the CSO had not been understood until this point. In the words of the Director:

It's not something out there, external [the values-indicator framework]. It gives us a place, encourages us, respects our identity.... So we appropriate ourselves into the indicators, make them our own. We had to feel that the indicators were ours; that we are the scale, and that's how it's been most useful to us: not something external which is going to measure us, but something internal which will help us improve our interrelationships with the community and nature.

(Interview notes, 6 June 2010, quoted in Podger *et al.* 2013: 20)

The academic researchers worked in a similar way to develop assessment methods which were consistent with the nature of the activities being evaluated. Since Echeri was centred on creative and artistic programmes, it was clear that assessment methods should engage the youth in a similar way, rather than, for example, surveys, questionnaires or interviews. In anticipation, the academics had already produced a draft handbook of 35 assessment methods and tools to serve as a 'menu' or library that the CSO could choose from and be stimulated by. (Types of assessment method are covered in more detail in Chapter 5.)

This led to the co-design of localized assessment methods that adapted standard and rigorous assessment tools, such as scale surveys, supplemented with qualitative assessment tools to measure the 22 indicators selected. For example, as already mentioned, a spatial survey was devised in which respondents could vote by moving into different physical spaces: a large spiral of different coloured scarves was constructed on the ground and each colour associated with one of the three points on the response scale (a little –more or less – a lot). This was both about not assuming written literacy, and about working within the existing framework of the group, as an arts-oriented practice (Figure 3.1). When questions were read out, the youth went to the colour that best reflected their response. We were able to record the responses of individual youth (assisted by video recording), and aggregated results and patterns for the group as a whole. In order to explore the underlying reasons for some responses, we followed up with focus group discussions – which also enabled us to triangulate the data, through a mixed mode approach (Taylor and Bogdan 1998).

The CSO practitioners had no previous conception of mixed methods approaches, but adopted them easily. Amezcua-Luna told us:

The value of this [mixed methods approach] for me was that we could assess how the group was doing, but also how each individual was positioned within the group. This is very, very important. It was supplemented by the focus group, and that was very important. After noting where everybody was [in a spatial survey], we asked them questions like 'why do you feel valued a lot', etc. For me, that went beyond the number, and gave me all the invisible information. But the numerical aspect was as important as the qualitative, because it provided a vision of the whole, it gave us strategies for the whole group.

(Ibid.: 20)

It should be noted that the effectiveness – and ease – of operationalizing indicator measurements, was more uneven with some of the other groups in the field trials; the complexities of relationships between indicators and qualitative or quantitative forms of measurement will be returned to in Chapter 5.

With Echeri, the co-partnering and the degree of mutual education and reciprocity worked very well with complete collaboration on the design of assessment methods. This process of co-developing assessment tools was also characterized by flexibility and iterative improvement. For the school's programme, for example, the spatial survey presented logistical challenges with large groups. There was also concern about imitation bias and in-group bias, group conformity bias (Jetten, Spears, and Manstead 1996) and social desirability response bias (Arnold and Feldma 1981; Furnham 1986). In each of these cases, participants might be unduly influenced by others, or by social norms, in ways that might distort the accuracy of findings.

Accordingly, the researchers devised a new method, which required the youth to answer the questions by adopting certain body postures (corporeal survey): standing with raised arms for 'a lot', with hands on hips for 'more or less', lying on the floor to represent 'a little'. To reduce imitation and group conformity biases, the children were asked to close eyes and adopt postures at the sound of a drum beat. Other assessment methods included word elicitation via hand painting (depicting emotions felt at the end of a project – Figure 3.2) and tests of knowledge using drama.

The final intended outcome of testing the prototype values-indicator toolkit was about its usefulness to CSOs in having appropriate and acceptable performance metrics to share with funders. This was effective with Echeri Consultores. Their major funder, Reforestamos Mexico, was involved in the field study. Their representative suggested getting the youth to do a hand-painting circle, and that was turned into a word elicitation task. Painting each other's hands gives the youth a starting point to talk about the emotions that they felt when they finished a reforestation project:

> They could name emotions, like happy, joyful, but they also said some beautiful things. A 12-year-old boy said he felt that he had left a positive footprint on the world. After doing the reforestation, he was helping to 'prevent the world from falling sick'. Then a small six-year-old boy painted the entire hand green and when asked to talk about it, he just said 'I feel green!'
>
> (Interview notes with Amezcua-Luna, quoted in WeValue 2015: 5)

Despite the specificity of indicators and measures to the local context, the clarity and consistency of the results gave Echeri considerable leverage with funders. Amezcua-Luna was invited to Mexico City to speak to the General Manager, the Head of Fundraising and the Head of Research from their funding organisation Reforestamos Mexico. The collaborative evaluation with ESDinds enabled her to persuade Reforestamos Mexico to reconceptualise the work of

Figure 3.2 Illustration of a localized measurement for a local indicator: hand painting to illustrate emotional connections to the community of life.

Source: photograph provided with permission, by Cardiela Amezcua Luna.

Echeri as something of international relevance, rather than just a local project (ibid.). In fact, it was precisely because Echeri could both measure and persuasively communicate their social and ethical impacts that they achieved further funding. This was during a time of cuts, when Reforestamos Mexico projects were cut from 42 to only 20.

What we learnt: significant lessons from the field

The Echeri field trial was initially a pilot study to test the hypothesis that suitable assessment tools could be devised for some, if not all, of the draft indicators. However, through this process, some crucially important and more general issues were opened up – about framing relationships between values and indicators; about varieties of collaboration and engagement; and about what counts as validity. As already noted, this was about more than minor adjustments to the overall toolkit and its associated participatory processes. It had become clear that there were also profound results for the project overall, each of which is briefly outlined below, and will then be described in greater depth and extended in the following chapter 'Issues in making values tangible'.

First, we learnt that explicitly developing a shared understanding of intangible social values was not just a matter of measurement, but enabled the *elicitation* of agreed values that might previously have remained implicit and vague; generated the *crystallisation* for individuals and groups of what their values are and how their achievement might be assessed; and increased the effective *communication* of these within and across an organization. Thus, the use of our values-based approach caused substantive transformational learning within this CSO. Importantly, individual participants, for example, changed their behaviour once shared values had been articulated and absorbed through discussion. As Amezcua-Luna explains:

> It was not so much an issue of 'this specific indicator influenced me in this way' – rather, the process helped them to identify values in action. Based on what values, they take what decisions? For example, one youth, 'Carlos', was a good example of 'before and after'. He is mid-way through the age range and beginning to participate a lot more. He used to be very unfocused, but after the process and specifically through the exercise, it allowed him to identify where he was. Now he participates, relates more, has more leadership.
>
> (Interview notes, 18 May 2010, quoted in Podger *et al.* 2013: 24)

These positive and transformational impacts also enabled the participants to be more confident in taking their values in action forward as a team:

> the youth went to a residential camp for environmental youth at the national level, with seven different indigenous ethnic groups from across the country, all from priority areas for biodiversity. The Juatarhu youth, without me, ran the same process for other youth. They offered it as an ice-breaker activity, an integration game. It was the first time they met, and there were different languages, cultures, etc. They did a spiral of 'where are you?' [i.e. spatial survey using a spiral] – they chose four indicator questions and asked them, using the spiral. At that meeting they chose the National Council and five out of the 11 youth were elected from Juatarhu. That was an indirect result [of the project's] – empowerment. The indicator process is very empowering to youth.
>
> (Ibid.: 24)

For Echeri as an organization, involvement in the field trial created bonding and informed action as well as increasing both critical and tacit knowledge. It enabled what had been previously intangible shared values to be more explicitly stated and acted on. Through deep and critical engagement with the values-based toolkit they were able to generate their own effective performance measurements about the preferred outcomes of their programs; which, in turn, had positive effects on their funders.

Second, this led to a reframing of how a values-based toolkit could be offered to groups. We moved from fore-fronting values to starting from indicators; and from defining these as value statements, to articulating them as a 'pool' – a range of triggers from which groups could develop their own, specific and localized concepts, priorities and relationships. This meant that, rather than being a toolkit as we had originally envisaged, the process was increasingly understood as a system; one that contains the set of elicitation elements, but needs to be adjusted by each group.

This, in turn, produced the final significant lesson for the researchers; an increased understanding that groups would not only customize their own values, indicators and the relationships between these, but would also have different intentions in articulating shared social values, depending on the outputs desired. A values-based approach enables opportunities to increase bonding and belonging, or to highlight gaps and differences in perception. It can be aimed mainly at external stakeholders, or at internal group learning. Thus, some organisations will emphasize elicitation for 'discovery and clarification' of values being used in action: whilst others might focus on developing measurable indicators, to support funding applications. Working with organisations to reach a shared understanding of what their central evaluation goals are thus needed to also become part of our system.

In the next part, we will explore in greater depth the many implications of this learning; how it changed a focus on evaluation methods to one concerned with enabling processes for transformational learning; what kinds of participatory evaluation methods best engage and empower participants; and how to be sure that the shared intangible values indicators expressed by a group are valid, comparable and transferable.

References

Arnold, H. J. and Feldman, D. C. (1981) 'Social Desirability Response Bias in Self-Report Choice Situations', *Academy of Management Journal*, 24(2), pp. 377–385.

Burford, G., Velasco, I., Janouskova, S., Zahradnik, M., Hak, T., Podger, D., Piggot, G., and Harder, M. K. (2013) 'Field Trials of a Novel Toolkit for Evaluating "Intangible" Values-related Dimensions of Projects', *Evaluation and Program Planning*, 36(1), pp. 1–14.

ESDinds. (2011) *The development of indicators and assessment tools for CSO projects promoting values-based education for sustainable development. Deliverable No. 17: Project final report* (amended version, resubmitted 23 September 2011). Available at: www.esdinds. eu/resources.

Furnham, A. (1986) 'Response Bias, Social Desirability and Dissimulation', *Personality and Individual Differences*, 7(3), pp. 385–400.

Harder, Marie K., Velasco, I., Burford, G., Podger, D., Janoušková, S., Piggot, G., and Hoover, E. (2014) 'Reconceptualizing "Effectiveness" in Environmental Projects: Can We Measure Values-Related Achievements?' *Journal of Environmental Management*, 139, pp. 120–134.

Jetten, J., Spears, R., and Manstead, A. S. R. (1996) 'Intergroup Norms and Intergroup Discrimination: Distinctive Self-Categorization and Social Identity Effects', *Journal of Personality and Social Psychology*, 71(6), pp. 1222–1233.

Kemmis, S. (2001) Exploring the Relevance of Critical Theory for Action Research in the Footsteps of Jurgen Habermas. In Reason, P. and Bradbury, H. (Eds.) *Handbook of Action Research: Participative Inquiry and Practice* (pp. 91–103). London: SAGE.

Lather, P. (1986) 'Research as Praxis', *Harvard Educational Review*, 56(3), pp. 257–278.

Podger, D., Velasco, I., Amezcua Luna, C., Burford, G., and Harder, M. K. (2013) 'Can Values Be Measured? Significant Contributions from a Small Civil Society Organisation Through Action Research Evaluation', *Action Research*, 11, pp. 8–30. Available at: http://arj.sagepub.com/content/early/2012/12/04/1476750312467833.

Taylor, S. J. and Bogdan, R. (1998) *Introduction to Qualitative Research Methods: A Guidebook and Resource* (3rd edn). Hoboken, NJ: John Wiley & Sons Inc.

WeValue (2015) *Understanding and Evaluating Intangible Impacts of Projects or Organisations* University of Brighton. Retrieved from https://cpb-eu-w2.wpmucdn.com/blogs. brighton.ac.uk/dist/d/1992/files/2016/03/WE-VALUE-shorter-toolkit_2015-1aam0zp. pdf.

Part II

Key themes in measuring intangible social values

4 Issues in making values tangible

As outlined in the previous chapter, the co-research work with Echeri enabled several moments of illumination and inspiration. Most crucially, the results from this field study led to a shift away from attempting to pre-define generic and generalizable value headings or their proto-indicators. Instead we started exploring how they could trigger local conversations to *elicit* and *crystallise*, as well as eventually measure. It was becoming clear that the value-based *process* itself was very important in enabling groups to learn about themselves, to bond better together, to build a stronger and more united vision, even to develop improved individual self-esteem and confidence and to potentially transform themselves as organizations. It was also leading to more explicit visions and identities derived from the effects of the participants' mainstreaming their new, shared, values vocabulary, which also generated a language for communicating this to funders and enabled alliance-building with other groups.

Second, Echeri showed us that we should move away from our original sequential process that went from values and then to the associated indicators, and instead start from a *pool* of all the indicators, and let the group members connect their chosen ones to their uniquely identified broader values. (Podger *et al.* 2010). The framework offered to Echeri for action research and critical review had been co-developed and devised by the EU-funded consortium of CSOs plus university researchers, but it still had design features from traditional academia implicit in it: in particular, the concept that Echeri would first choose the values of relevance to it, out of an already defined and generalizable core list of six, and work with the affiliated indicators for each. The field trail started with this approach. However, when reviewing the project, Echeri started explaining their different view of the structural relationships between values (as described in the previous chapter). This prompted us to ask ourselves to what extent those relationships challenged our toolkit-based framework. It was already understood by academia that some indicators might be useful to more than one value, but here was a sign of something much more interesting: could the indicators, if all pooled together, be useful for a CSO to construct their own set to measure their own first-choice value – even one not on the initial list of six? The field trials thus led to the generation of new knowledge, which was later seen to be significant. Through action research and in their context, Echeri drew out the fact that not only would some of the indicators (e.g. for Care and Respect) also work for Diversity but in fact a combination from the pooled indicators could even be used for their own core values of Friendship or Humility – even though these were not in the original six values offered.

Finally, this case study began to help clarify issues around validity. This was a decisive move from abstraction and generality to localization and specificity. Moving away from attempting to define generic value-indicators and towards working with indicators that elicit and crystallise as well as measure, does not mean that the resulting statements are just 'personal' or 'relative'. The underlying process – despite being 'fuzzy' – is of systematic and rigorous construct definition. CSOs can be strongly encouraged to translate indicators into their own internal language, effectively using them as templates for the construction of their own values and measurement tools. To take an example; a group of people within a civil society organization (CSO) might define the value of 'empowerment' inter-subjectively by listing those behaviours and attitudes that would constitute success (or, at least, progress) in their specific 'youth empowerment' project. Of course, this result could never be a fully comprehensive, totally objective definition of empowerment; nor would it resemble the various theoretical constructs of empowerment as reviewed by Herbert *et al.* (2009) for example.[1] Yet, as a definition achieved through an implicit process and group consensus, it is more than just the sum of individual perspectives. It is a clearly articulated, inter-subjective, and most importantly, useful definition that can form a basis for measuring the extent to which empowerment has been achieved – in every sense that matters to the CSO – within the project in question. Its strength is precisely in its context-specificity and *localization*. What matters is the clear validity of this group consensus – the ability of a CSO director to tell donors, for example, that 'we are all agreed that *this* is an indicator of *empowerment* in our own project'. In this sense, every shortlist of indicators has inherent item validity for the group members, provided that the participatory process used to generate it is an adequate one. That is, each indicator is measuring what it purports to measure. This crucial issue of validity will be explored in greater depth in Chapter 6.

In addition, organizations could self-define what they wanted out of this process of eliciting, crystalizing and measuring their values and its particular relevance to their current and future plans. The process was in fact enabling different kinds of relevance to groups, for example by focusing on organizational clarification and validation, and/or on monitoring and evaluation, or on strategic planning and/or on group bonding. The case study chapters in Part III give examples where groups used our values-based framework for many different aims and outcomes, from internal organizational capacity-building, to uncovering and being able to describe the multitude of a project's legacies.

These insights of course led to new questions. Should values-in-practice proto-indicators, when pooled from the existing values and indicator lists, be presented grouped in a particular category (biased by the researchers), or randomly? Could the way they were presented lead to confusions over what type of evaluation was being done? And if what matters to people within a given CSO is that, for example, '[youth] feel they are treated equitably and with fairness', should this be classified by researchers as a process or as an impact of the project[2] – or indeed did it matter? How did the participatory process need to be changed to ensure good design? Did the 'toolkit' need to be modified for different users or contexts (and would this affect validity)? What would we/could we learn from the other field trials?

Values and subjectivity

Another major question to arise was the nature of the CSO values: were they objective or subjective? Although the original values development and process design had followed a grounded theory perspective, the prototype toolkit and process resulting from the first phase of the research had actually resulted in an instrument that was conceptually not dissimilar to more traditional operationalizations of values (e.g. Rokeach, 1973; House, Hanges, Javidan, Dorfman, and Gupta, 2004; Peterson, Park, and Seligman, 2005; Schwartz, 2007). In other words, the proto-type toolkit sent out for the field-testing phase contained a predetermined construct of each value, albeit multidimensional, understood to be effectively covered by a set of 20–40 associated indicators of behaviours and perspectives. There were, however, two key differences from the conventional approaches mentioned above: first that the indicators were not associated to a specific assessment method, such as a survey; and second that the indicators were not considered definitive, but provisional. Thus, the operational starting point for the field-testing was a set of pre-defined indicators that were subject to local selection and possibly addition and even modification, with built-in flexibility intended to allow them to be easily adaptable to a wide range of quantitative and qualitative instruments, to be defined in accordance with local suitability.

During the second phase of the research the six values and their associated indicators were tested with three other organizations besides Echeri – Italy (Lush cosmetics company), Sierra Leone (Red Cross child combatant rehabilitation programme) and Germany (People's Theater peer education project) – deliberately chosen as a diverse set of organizations. Surprisingly, the indicators derived by the original consortium members, which were linked by their sustainability agenda, proved to be remarkably transferable in every one of these new contexts. In each case almost all of the indicators were locally considered relevant, useful and important (Podger *et al.* 2013). But it was also true that in some of these other field trials, the CSOs naturally considered the indicators as linked to different values than the original six, just as Echeri had. We then hypothesized that the indicators might be more useful to CSOs if presented as a single 'pooled' list, recognizing that it would be a long one (177 in total). In the field studies, most of the CSOs also found discussing the values label words (e.g. Trust) relatively difficult, as there were always many different interpretations, even within a given group, and these did not settle to a consensus but usually

kept shifting in the session. Discussion thus could become focused on attempting to align different understandings of these value-labels and defining what the
concepts 'meant', rather than on finalizing a list of relevant ones. Discussions of
the indicators, on the other hand, were usually much more straightforward, producing a prompt consensus of localized expressions. It therefore turned out to be
much more useful to start with the pooled indicator list, asking the CSOs to
mark out those important to them, and later to draw out what values label words
they represented to that CSO. This may sound like a small change, but conceptually it is very significant, as it suggests that the vocabulary associated with
values may be too elusive, dynamic and nuanced to be useful across and within
different groups, whereas specific indicators, developed as expressions of values-
in-practice, are more clearly communicated and agreed upon.

It was in Mexico, however, that the process of field-testing really took on a
new dimension. As well as the Echeri experience already discussed, work with
Guanajuato University took the issue of vocabulary further. As the head of its
sustainability unit reviewed the indicators, she found them, in common with all
this phase of field trials, highly relevant and useful, and the values to which they
were associated likewise useful, with no objection to any of the value label
words. What was suggestive, however, is that in addition to the value constructs
the EU team had developed, it was felt that the indicators resonated with *other
value constructs* – not just other value terms or synonyms or variants – which
also belonged to that unit's own internal priority values. It was here that that
more signs emerged that the indicators originally developed from a set of only
six values could in fact be applied to completely new values. This meant decon-
structing the value-indicator associations developed in the first phase of the
research, and while keeping the existing indicators, reordering them to generate
new and different value constructs. The idea was to 'pick and mix', from this list
of over 100 indicators, so as to find the ones that fitted and formed a representation of a particular group's pre-existing values.

In the second field visit to Guanajuato University's sustainability unit, the
research question in terms of this discussion was: can the indicators be associated to values different from those out of which they were originally derived?
The answer was clear. The staff at Guanajuato University had no difficulty
whatsoever connecting the indicators to their own preferred value label words.
These were generally a very different vocabulary to that used for the values list
generated by the original consortium. Furthermore and importantly, different
groups within the Guanajuato University sustainability unit were able, without
controversy, to agree on assignations of shared values to the specific behaviours
and attitudes denoted by the indicators from the pool, which acted as 'elements'
of those values. In other words, the process was now efficient, easily used and
worthwhile – but it used statements to 'construct' local values concepts. And
the concepts contained in those elements (proto-indicators) seemed transferable – while the values labels were not.

Values, from this perspective, may be considered not as objective, concrete,
mutually independent entities which are expressed through behaviour and

attitudes; but as subjective, interpretive categories that are assigned to such behaviour and attitudes, giving them meaning (c.f. Debats and Bartelds, 1996). What is most important, from the perspective of evaluators seeking to quantify or at least crystallize intangible values-based dimensions of projects, is that the indicators function as an effective, external anchor for generating inter-subjective (shared) ethical interpretations and vocabularies, in the form of assigned values. Our fieldwork clearly illustrates that in order for this approach to work, values categories should not be externally imposed on the indicators. If they are, the evaluation would lose both its subjective (individual) validations and its inter-subjective (shared) validation. What would be measured would be the researchers' own value constructs.

This might suggest that traditional approaches to the measurement of values, through theory-based value constructs that then become operationalized in standardized surveys – for all their operational validity – may have a validity gap in terms of the credibility criterion outlined above. Such surveys might be said to measure, not 'a given value' (since values appear not to be definite entities), but merely one particular construct designed by the researchers and imposed on the respondents. Our values-based approach addresses this challenge by giving space for participants' subjective value assignations to become inter-subjective (shared) through dialogue. The indicator framework, by focusing the initial attention on specific behaviours and attitudes, ensures that the process does not become overly abstract and hence irrelevant for practical evaluation purposes. What is ultimately 'measured', then, is the group's own inter-subjective consensus of what constitutes a specific value, anchored in measurable, commonly observable external expressions in the form of behaviours, perceptions or indirect measures. This, in turn, raises another issue; what are the relationships between what people say and what they do?

Linking values with actions

In the introduction to this book we defined values as ideas about what is desirable, enduring beliefs about a preferred condition or behaviour, and criteria about what should happen. However, precisely because such values are often intangible, there is not only a problem of articulating and negotiating them explicitly, but also of being able to demonstrate that articulated values connect to real actions. That is, people may publicly espouse particular values, but do not always behave in ways usually associated with those values. This has been called the 'value-action gap' (Blake 1999). Because the values we hold are often less then fully conscious they can be about what we feel rather than what we think or can explain. Entrenched habits and routines, unconsidered common-sense beliefs and intuitions, personal emotions, and situational cues can influence which values are recognized and prioritized; and can have contradictory effects. In one of our projects, for example, to develop a toolkit of values-based indicators for secondary schools for pro-environmental behaviours (Burford *et al.* 2015) a key element was exploring how to bridge value-action gaps. This work – covered in more detail in the Chapter 9 case study – was to see if the value-indicators framework could be a means to simulate collective reflection of, and understandings about, relationships between values, discourse and action.

The previous field trials had already indicated that it was possible to strengthen particular values through articulating them in words, sharing and discussing them with others, and thus reflecting on one's own beliefs and behaviours. As Maio *et al.* have put it:

> We believe that … generating reasons for a value provides concrete reasons of why behaving consistently with the value is sensible and justified. Thus, when situational forces work against pro-value behavior, people become able to retrieve concrete information in addition to their vague feelings about the value.
>
> (2001: 14)

Explicitly eliciting, clarifying and crytallizing values, then, moves people from the affective realm to the cognitive, and hence enables a more direct understanding of links to behaviours and actions (see also Dixon 1978; Schlater and Sontag 1994).

As Rescher (1982) writes, value subscription can manifest itself both through *discourse* (what people say) and through overt *action* (what they do), but the critical test of value presence is consistency between the two. Citing Rescher's work, Schlater and Sontag offer two contrasting examples of inconsistency: 'A person may "talk" the value but not implement it in action, or a person may act in accordance with a value but not subscribe to it verbally' (1994: 5).

This is not just about individuals, then, but has important implications for organizational learning and behaviour as well. Organizations also have implicit values that may not be obvious or may be contradictory; as well as gaps between what formal strategies and policies say, and their actual implementation on the ground. By having processes for articulating, negotiating and measuring intangible values CSOs can go beyond the successful achievement of users' self-selected evaluation goals. In addition, they can identify value-action gaps, design possible behaviour change or new actions to close these gaps and/or enable the implementation of change towards a more aligned value-action relationship. The aim, then, is not merely more explicit values, or more explicit actions, but an increased, explicit and transparent consistency between individual and group values and actions.

From toolkit to system

Through the actual implementation of the original two-year ESDinds project, a design process with five broad steps emerged. Because the overall approach encouraged a localized 'dialogue of values' (Maturana and Varela 1991), the exact nature, sequence and relative importance of these steps can differ from one organization to another, depending on their primary purpose for using the approach. In fact, what the values-based approach can offer for self-learning may turn out to be more important than for evaluation or assessment.

This meant that, rather than being a toolkit as we had originally envisaged, the process was increasingly understood as a framework or system; one that contains the following elements, but needs to be adjusted for each group depending on the outputs desired. Some will find it more useful to emphasise elicitation e.g. for 'discovery and clarification' of values being used in action: others might focus on developing measurable indicators. We suggest five steps.

Elicitation

The initial step is the elicitation of local, contextualized statements of 'what is important' to group members – at a moderately superficial level in terms of what comes to mind at first hand. This elicitation, or triggering or drawing out, can be done using direct questions, or storytelling, or using pictures or objects that demonstrate areas of importance to individual members. It can be done in a corporate, artistic, creative, serious or playful manner. Basically, each individual expresses, by using a photo for example, which acts as a prompt and prop, something valuable, meaningful and/or worthwhile to them. This approach automatically encourages specific examples and generalisations of them, e.g. 'the rainbow reminded me of ... which is what we do a lot of, actually'.

Using 'trigger statements'

Second, a reference list of 'trigger statements' (also known as proto-indicators or indicators once they are contextualized) are used to facilitate participants to think beyond their usual boundaries. These are short, concise statements about what other people have said are 'worthwhile, meaningful or valuable to them' about their work or membership in groups. An example might be: 'We see mistakes as an opportunity to learn'. Group members will easily identify some statements that represent what they already think – or adapt similar ones. But they will also be 'triggered' to bring out previously undeveloped values, that is, already held but not explicitly articulated. In some cases this can cause an 'aha' moment as participants recognize something about themselves they did not previously explicitly know. In this step, individuals read through a list of 125–166 values statements, without discussion, and mark the top 15–20 which especially resonate strongly with them.

This list of proto-indicators is offered as a 'pool', with no mention of any specific connection to different values headings such as 'Trust' or 'Equity'. Instead, at a later stage, participants move around their own statements (on cards on the table) into naturally forming sets, and often give those sets value headings similar to our original terms. In other words, participants go on to 'construct' their own values headers around their chosen list, rather than construct 'lists' of indicators under their (rarely agreed) values headers. Furthermore, the wording of the 'trigger statements' has come from field data with as little change in the working as possible, which seems to make them intuitive for users – compared to externally derived lists of other methods which often use formal language and formats that users find difficult to relate to. One interesting result is that while choosing their values statements, the participants do not distinguish between them in the manner of any common classification systems in evaluation or indicator literature. For example, indicator 'types' in a formal UN classification include 'process' or 'impact', but we have some statements that have been chosen as a process indicator in one group, but as an impact in another.

Developing a new shared vocabulary

Individuals have now marked which of the 'trigger list' values statements resonate with their feelings of what is valuable, meaningful and worthwhile about their membership and work. Next, the facilitator invites a member to read out and explain one of their choices – and then asks others to comment, expound, give counter examples etc., to get a general discussion going. Usually, the conversation dies down when people have given sufficient illustrations and counter-illustrations of their interpretations for everyone to be satisfied with the latest interpretation of the statement. At that point, the facilitator asks for the statement to be summarized on a card and placed on the table – with whatever wording the group are comfortable with. Sometimes up to 3–4 different 'triggers' can be brought into one conversation, with the implications on meaning of minute changes in wording or emphasis being explored: the group is getting to know itself. Often the final, localized statement is a variation on one of the triggers, or lies between 2–3 of them: much less commonly is there an effectively new values statement. This continues until all the chosen statements are covered, and the facilitator has checked for any 'missing' concepts: usually 12–18 values statements are left on the table.

Organising: towards articulating underpinning values

With facilitator guidance, the group can now physically, spatially organise on the table the localized values statements they have negotiated and agreed upon which can in future be used effectively as local indicators. For example, several might be grouped together and labelled 'how we support each other', while another might be fundamental principles they start with, and yet another the 'social improvements we seek'. These structured cards sometimes have tree-like structures: sometimes like foundations, pillars and roofs of buildings; sometimes haphazard. But they all have deep local meaning. And often there are comments of surprise: that the overarching goals illustrated are indeed what they think of in daily work but … not what is on their website. Or, that they now see why they like empowerment projects, but not training ones: the priorities of the values-in-action of the group are being well captured in this bespoke 'Values Framework' which they have constructed. It can be used to guide them more 'truly' in future work.

Developing measurable indicators

Some groups are not interested in measuring anything: the framework up to this stage is enough. But by negotiating quite concise local values statements, with reference to actions that the group is familiar with, they have already pre-prepared them as good indicators. Importantly, the level of detail and contextualisation in each must be not too great or small in order to take these forward as indicators: that aspect is best coordinated through an experienced facilitator.

Each of those concise statements can now easily be tied to specific actions that can be observed or recorded or measured with proxies: in some cases by rule of thumb, and in some cases with multiple methods and contexts to achieve triangulation, depending on the measurement purpose and need of the CSO. These measures can be compared over time, or converted into Likert scales like 'red, amber, green' or '1, 2, 3, 4, 5', and different topics can be chosen for special examination in different years. The academic facilitators can help develop rigorous measure method combinations suited for external inquiries, or perhaps less rigorous but quick ones for internal feedback.

What may not be obvious, and indeed was an unexpected finding, is that through all our studies we found that the localizations tended to be minor and each particular indicator was still identifiable and separate from other indicators on the reference 'trigger list'. This means that localised indicators, and their related measures, could still be compared across organisations: the approach had some transferability and generalizability. The results for a particular indicator across different organisations might look very different (e.g. surveys versus interviews versus observations), and have to be considered individually or converted to different types of scaling techniques but they all measured the same concept. Although the initial intention was that the results must be considered valid to each CSO, it seemed they could also be valid across CSOs.

Implications for action research and evaluation

Our co-development of a values-based evaluation approach thus had impacts beyond the significant modifications they created for our initial prototype toolkit for CSO self-evaluation. The lessons we learned along the way also provide preliminary evidence of something much bigger: that the current general vacuum around intangible social values-based indicators – thought to be unavoidable and inevitable – can actually be filled as long as key principles such as unitary validity is maintained. The use of values-based indicators could in principle then be extended to other domains: the impact of any values approach could be measured against other approaches, and values outcomes against other outcomes such as monetary, environmental, and/or educational (knowledge) outcomes. The approach offered here, then, allows local specificity whilst also enabling comparability across 'locals'. The system could be used for measuring many different CSOs – for example, charities all funded by one funder, or for developing measuring systems that can work across organizations which have local, national and international levels.

Our findings on relationships between values and indicators also has potential to change fundamental ideas in values measurement work which currently treats values as having equivalent structures. And our finding that the use of peer-elicited values-based indicator lists such as ours might cause substantive and time-efficient transformative learning (see more in Chapter 8) is relevant to sustainable development and education for sustainable development, as well as mainstream management areas such as organizational change (ESDinds 2011).

Finally, by being enabled to measure things that have not previously been measured, such as indicators for trust, empowerment and integrity, a values-based approach also begins to communicate a new voice for society. This is because, being able to explicitly discuss a shared vocabulary for organisations from local to national and even global levels that go beyond directly monetary or performance assessments enables social values and ethics to take a more central place in decision-making and transformational social action.

Notes

1 Herbert *et al.* (2009) refer to theoretical definitions of empowerment by Rappaport (1981, 1987), Perkins and Zimmerman (1985), Gutierrez, DeLois, and GlenMaye (1995), and Anderson, Funnell, Fitzgerald, and Marrero (2000).
2 During the qualitative content analysis phase, we had classified every emerging proto-indicator according to the UNESCO typology, respectively as a baseline, content, process, learning, output, outcome, impact or performance indicator; but at the Core Group Meeting, the CSO partners unanimously agreed that they did not find this typology at all useful.

References

Anderson, R. M., Funnell, M. M., Fitzgerald, J. T., and Marrero, D. G. (2000). 'The Diabetes Empowerment Scale: A Measure of Psychosocial Self-Efficacy', *Diabetes Care*, 23, pp. 739–743.

Blake, J. (1999) 'Overcoming the "Value-Action Gap" in Environmental Policy: Tensions Between National Policy and Local Experience', *Local Environment* 4(3), pp. 257–278.

Burford, G, Hoover, E, Dahl, A, and Harder, M. K. (2015). 'Making the Invisible Visible: Designing Values-Based Indicators and Tools for Identifying and Closing "Value Action Gaps"'. In Didham, R. J., Doyle, D., Klein, J., and Thoresen, V. W. (Eds.) *Responsible Living: Concepts, Education and Future Perspectives*. Berlin Heidelberg: Springer Verlag, 113–134.

Debats, D. L. and Bartelds, B. F. (1996). *The Structure of Human Values: A Principal Components Analysis of the Rokeach Value Survey (RVS)*. Retrieved from http://dissertations.ub.rug.nl/FILES/faculties/pps w/1996/d.l.h.m.debats/c5.pdf.

Dixon, B. R., (1978) *An investigation into the use of Raths' values clarification strategies with grade eight pupils* (Doctoral dissertation, Michigan State University, 1978). Dissertation Abstracts International 39:5987A.

ESDinds (2011) *ESDinds: The development of values-based indicators and assessment tools for civil society organizations promoting education for sustainable development. Deliverable 17: final project report to European Commission Seventh Framework Programme* (FP7/2007–2013), www.esdinds.eu. ESDinds Project Consortium led by University of Brighton, UK.

Gutierrez, L. M., DeLois, K. A., and GlenMaye, L. (1995). 'Understanding Empowerment Practice: Building on Practitioner-Based Knowledge', *Families in Society*, 76, pp. 534–542.

Herbert, R. J., Gagnon, A. J., Rennick, J. E., and O'Loughlin, J. L. (2009). 'A Systematic Review of Questionnaires Measuring Health-Related Empowerment', *Research and Theory for Nursing Practice: An International Journal*, 23, pp. 107–132.

House, R. J., Hanges, P. J., Javidan, M., Dorfman, P. W., and Gupta, V. (2004). *Culture, Leadership and Organizations: The GLOBE Study of 62 Societies*. Thousand Oaks, CA: Sage Publications.

Maio, G. R, Olson, J. M, Allen, L., and Bernard M. M. (2001). 'Addressing Discrepancies Between Values and Behavior: The Motivating Effect of Reasons', *Journal of Experimental Social Psychology*, 37(2), pp. 104–117.

Maturana, H., and Varela, F. J. (1991) *Autopoiesis and Cognition: The Realization of the Living*. Dordrecht, the Netherlands: D. Reidel Publishing Company.

Perkins, D. D., and Zimmerman, M. A. (1985). 'Empowerment Theory, Research, and Application', *American Journal of Community Psychology*, 23, pp. 569–579.

Peterson, C., Park, N., and Seligman, M. E. P. (2005). Assessment of Character Strengths. In Koocher, G. P., Norcross, J. C., and Hill III, S. S. (Eds.) *Psychologists' Desk Reference* (2nd edn). New York: Oxford University Press.

Podger, D., Piggot, G., Zahradnik, M., Janouskova, S., Velasco, I., Hak, T., Dahl, A., Jimenez, A., and Harder, M. K. (2010). 'The Earth Charter and the ESDinds Initiative: Developing Indicators and Assessment Tools for Civil Society Organisations to Examine the Values Dimensions of Sustainability Projects', *Journal of Education for Sustainable Development*, 4, pp. 297–305.

Podger, D., Velasco, I., Amezcua Luna, C., Burford, G., and Harder, M. K. (2013). 'Can Values Be Measured? Significant contributions from a Small Civil Society Organisation Through Action Research Evaluation', *Action Research*, 11(1), pp. 8–30.

Rappaport, J. (1981). 'In Praise of Paradox: A Social Policy of Empowerment Over Prevention', *American Journal of Community Psychology*, 9, pp. 1–25.

Rappaport, J. (1987). 'Terms of Empowerment/Exemplars of Prevention: Toward a Theory for Community Psychology', *American Journal of Community Psychology*, 15, pp. 121–148.

Rescher, N. (1982). *Introduction to Value Theory*. Lanham, MD: University Press of America.

Rokeach, M. (1973). *The Nature of Human Values*. The Free Press, New York

Schlater, J. D. and Sontag, M. (1994). 'Toward the Measurement of Human Values', *Family and Consumer Science Research Journal*, 23(1), pp. 4–25

Schwartz, S. H. (2007). Basic Human Values: Theory, Methods, and Applications. Retrieved from http://segr-did2.fmag.unict.it/Allegati/convegno%207-8-10-05/Schwartzpaper.pdf. Accessed 16 April 2018.

5 Designing processes
The criticality of deep participation

An important observation from the project work so far outlined, was that testing the prototype indicators in real evaluation contexts did not generate consistent impacts on the CSOs across all the field trials. As shown in Chapter 3, with Echeri, the fieldwork resulted not only in a re-envisioning of the meaning, significance and roles of evaluation, but also in a significant empowerment of youth participants, from 'service users' to co-evaluators and co-designers of their project. In others, the transformative effect was much less profound, and in at least one context, the trial appeared to have little or no lasting impact. Three other field study organisations and their characteristics are listed in Table 5.1. More detailed evaluation of their involvement can be found elsewhere (Burford et al. 2013). Here we want to work through a more general issue; how we found that the *form of participation*, and its levels of engagement, could have different impacts for the CSOs.

A realisation that process details were key

In meetings to review the field studies as they took place, project partners struggled to unpack the 'black box' of the toolkit they were developing, and understand what made the choosing, adapting and use of values-based indicators profoundly transformative in one context, yet largely ineffectual in another. Because of the implicit influence of pre-knowledge of traditional academic approaches to values measures which were focused on (predetermined) closed question queries with little interaction, it was some time before attention moved from the content of the 'toolkit' to its processes – the various interactions with the CSO members. The first clue came from the threefold process typology of Cox et al. (2007). Non-discipline-specific literature searches for 'process evaluation' unearthed their important paper, published in a specialist journal entitled *Work and Stress*. Alongside the conventional understanding of process evaluation as understanding 'what is done' within a project, i.e. the actual steps that comprise an intervention, the authors of this paper identified two additional layers of processes that were also able to be evaluated: (1) the organisational and social processes that constitute the wider context for the evaluation (*macro processes*); and (2) the specific ways in which the intervention is being managed

Table 5.1 Overview of the characteristics of the organizations involved in field studies, which were also later involved to retrospectively explore impacts of the WeValue workshop

Name of organization	Relationship to project consortium	Geographical and cultural setting	Type of organization
People's Theater	Full member of the consortium	Offenbach, Germany: youth volunteers	Small, independent local CSO inspired by the principles of the Bahá'í faith
PIMAUG (Environmental Institutional Programme of the University of Guanajuato)	Affiliate of the Earth Charter Initiative, a consortium member	Guanajuato, Mexico: university students	Cross-faculty environmental initiative within a university
Sierra Leone Red Cross Society (SLRCS) 'Youth as Agents of Behavioural Change' (YABC) Project	No relationship: initial connection made at conference hosted by a consortium member	Kabala, Sierra Leone: marginalized youth	National humanitarian society piloting a specific initiative designed by the International Federation of Red Cross and Red Crescent Societies (IFRC), a large international CSO

Source: adapted from Burford et al. (2013) 'Field Trials of a Novel Toolkit for Evaluating "Intangible" Vales-Related Dimensions of Projects', Evaluation and Program Planning, p. 36.

in a given situation (*implementation processes*). They argued that evaluating macro processes and implementation processes could provide vital clues to the age-old question of why an intervention that is highly successful in one context might fail in another. Our systematic research through design (RtD) approach, already outlined in the introduction to this book, enabled us not only to learn from this useful conceptual framework and apply it in our own work, but also to share our findings with more mainstream evaluation research and literature (Burford *et al.* 2013: 12).

While recognising the importance of macro processes and the wider context, we first focused our attention on implementation processes in each given situation, the most immediate problem to be understood better. Were different researchers actually engaging with the host organisations in different ways, and did something about these interactions have the potential to catalyse personal and organisational transformation? Other evaluation literature provided another crucial lead: stakeholders' experience of so-called 'process use' benefits of evaluation – that is, benefits accruing from the process of engaging in an evaluation rather than from its actual findings (Forss *et al.* 2002; Amo and Cousins 2007; Cousins 2007) – were found to be dependent on their *active participation* in designing and implementing the evaluation (Jacob *et al.* 2011). This resonated with our own observations: we quickly realised that the most successful field trials were those where not only the directors and project managers, but also frontline staff and even beneficiaries, had participated actively in choosing and adapting the indicators and tools that they wanted to use.

This led to a need to critically investigate our participation processes beyond the immediate demands of, and lessons learned for, our project. What would a participation framework look like, that whilst starting from designing evaluation methods suited to civil society organizations, would enable us to generate a robust, and more generally useful model? Could the outcomes from our case study trials inform this larger aim? This needed an extension to the central original research programme (of developing measures for CSO values which were valid to them), although there had also always been an intention of improving the guidelines for practitioners so that anyone who wanted to use our values-based framework could do so. Initial research investigations led first to the extensive and well-established literature on participatory evaluation and then beyond that to a broader examination of typologies of participation across multiple disciplines, including adaptive natural resource management, participatory community planning, and participatory design itself. After synthesizing and extending these concepts, our result was a novel four-dimensional conceptual framework for assessing participation. While relevant to all of the disciplines that had inspired it, as already noted we are particularly interested in engaging with research through design, precisely because our work matches its goals – an approach beyond disciplinary boundaries, that aims to create new socially purposeful knowledge (Harder *et al.* 2013). In addition, because these schematics helped so much with conceptualization for our own project, we recognized our need for their regular use, as well as their potential value to others.

In this chapter we outline this new way of thinking that clarifies concepts of participation, not just in terms of our own values-based project, and not only across diverse design areas but also across other disciplines that use participatory methods and processes, allowing clearer comparisons and cross-referencing. We see this clarification as a significant first step to remove multidisciplinary barriers to the productive building of a knowledge base around participation concepts. We suggest that design is the best field to lead this elimination of barriers, and we show specific connections to several other disciplines. The process outlined here attempts to develop a framework for mapping core underpinning (and usually implicit and unspoken) logics in the development of participatory processes. By revealing these hidden aspects in this way, the researcher can then become clearer about the implications of different kinds of participation, in terms of power, relationship-building and effectiveness.

Ideas about participation have been actively developed by designers for many years, through the separate traditions of user-centred design and participatory design, and more recently through various schools of co-design and human-centred design. All of these terms now carry multiple interpretations. The importance and role of the participation of 'others' in design has been debated in multiple contexts involving functionality, culture, usefulness, social responsibility, identity, design education and sustainability.[1] Yet consideration of participation is important not only within the field of design. Participation has become a focus of debate among academics and practitioners in very diverse fields. One driver is the growing numbers of peoples of the world who demand active involvement in the planning and implementation of initiatives affecting their lives. In the health sector, participatory approaches to both research (e.g. community-based participatory research) and service planning have become commonplace. In international development, 1980s discourses of participation have now become mainstream (Pretty *et al.* 1995; Guijt and Kaul Shah 1998). Sustainable development has embraced participation as a core ideal, both as a human rights issue and as a means of increasing the efficacy of interventions (Bell *et al.* 2012). Mainstream processes of formal monitoring and evaluation are also becoming more participatory, as non-governmental and civil society organizations take increasingly active roles in defining appropriate indicators and assessment strategies (Springett 2003; Crishna 2007). Even environmental management is now characterized by a more 'adaptive co-management' of natural resources (Ruitenbeek and Cartier 2001).

In most cases, conversations about participation were initiated at the periphery of disciplines (often as a reaction against 'top–down' practices). In the field of design, however, different aspects of participation have been under direct and conscious consideration for some time. Designers thus now have an opportunity to potentially lead new discussions across other fields, if they are able to draw together their understandings of participation into a consolidated knowledge base that can seed and stimulate ideas elsewhere. However, two significant difficulties we found in our inter-disciplinary study of participation are the diversity of approaches taken, and the lack of a common vocabulary for its characteristics. These might not at first appear obvious or problematic. But mainstream paradigms in education, social science, development studies, environmental management, evaluation, and business can impose invisible inherent constraints on both research and practice. For example, positivist epistemologies may frame researchers or consultants as 'experts' with a specialized knowledge that is inaccessible to 'others' (e.g. community stakeholders). This positivist perspective would imply that those 'others' should be studied objectively, and without the concept of participation. In different traditions, 'others' such as community stakeholders might be consulted up to a point, but their pre-existing ways of knowing and understanding the world are viewed as inferior to those of the 'experts'. Thus, consultants in the project evaluation might involve clients in localizing data collection tools to make them more palatable, but they are unwilling to modify their generalized (and externally derived) evaluation criteria to better reflect local consensus views on which project outcomes are actually meaningful.

Approaches such as those used in the work described in this book – action research, empowerment evaluation and co-design – directly counter the expert-centred approach. These perspectives actively blur distinctions between researcher, practitioner, and user. They are guided primarily by practical concerns, are sometimes explicitly grounded in stakeholders' ways of knowing, and are often aimed at building local capacity and catalyzing change. Thus, in different fields, discussions about different types of participation are emerging, but can too often end up being both discipline-specific, and unaware of their own particularities. The result is that the same vocabulary is sometimes used to refer to different concepts, and that researchers can repeatedly expend effort conceptualizing and communicating responses only focused on a specific situation. Instead of building increasingly higher-order concepts on foundations of earlier work, the result is a growing library of descriptive works that are not linked or generalized. In some cases, particularly in the design field, the mere act of participation can be seen as inherently valuable and progressive, so that formal and generalisable evaluation is not even considered. In addition, the low awareness of paradigm boundaries continues a lack of understanding across disciplines. Precisely for this reason, the cross-disciplinary design of participatory methods is needed, that can go beyond such boundaries. Particularly this needs to bridge the gap between the often narrative and project-based 'languages' of design and the more formal conceptualization, operationalization and quantitative measurements that characterize, for example, environmental management or educational studies.

The intention, then, is to first explore how to create a simple initial framework of generalized participation, organizing participation concepts so that they can be referred to more cleanly, with less confusion than is often present. This initial three-dimensional framework then allows us to illustrate the relationship of a fourth dimension – outputs evidence – as a sample for further development. We acknowledge our oversimplification for every category we use and concede that different categories, or indeed 'mosaics', are possible. In pragmatic terms, however, we believe our framework can free up concept-building about participation, which is currently stuck in a mire of mixed vocabulary and assumptions.

Relating aspects of participation across disciplines

In the field of participatory evaluation studies, increasing calls have been issued for the clearer conceptualization and operationalization of participation. Definitions of what is meant by participation are often vague and informal, and the term 'participatory evaluation' refers to a very diverse range of different scenarios. From their analysis of underpinning concepts, Daigneault and Jacob (2009) suggest conditions in each of three areas for an evaluation to be regarded as participatory: *control of the [evaluation] process, stakeholder diversity*, and *extent of involvement* (ibid.: 334). We use these conditions as our starting point, renaming them *depth, breadth* and *scope*:

- *Depth* is used in various works to refer to the *extent of control over decision-making* by the stakeholders (ibid.: 342; see also Hart 1992; Naylor *et al.* 2002).
- *Breadth* refers to the *diversity* of stakeholders invited to participate, that is, including decision-makers or clients for example (Bradley Cousins *et al.* 1996; Cornwall and Jewkes 1995; Daigneault and Jacob 2009).
- *Scope* refers to the *various stages* of key decision-making (Daigneault and Jacob 2009: 338) which can be categorized as initiation, design, implementation, reflection and communication.[2]

The first project where we used these concepts was a study of indigenous participation in intercultural education (Burford *et al.* 2012). Here, we conceptualized differing depths of participation as indicating differing power relationships between stakeholders of a lower status (e.g. indigenous community members) and higher status actors (e.g. conventionally trained educators). We categorized these relationships from what might be seen as the lowest – least participatory and most powerless – levels for the community as denigration (Level (–1)) and neglect (Level 0), through to an increasing equality of relationship, that is through acknowledgement/'learning about' (Level 1), engagement/'learning from' (Level 2), interculturality/'learning together' (Level 3), and full partnership/'learning as one' (Level 4). We found it useful to portray these levels schematically, as in Table 5.2. Here, typical processes, attitudes, assumptions and actions are correlated through example statements with the different potential levels of participation outlined above; in order to offer a systematic and comparative framework for articulating the range of *extent of control over decision-making* by the various stakeholders; that is, the depth of participation.

Note that in proposing such a typology, we do not mean to imply that a continuum is not useful, nor that higher levels are always preferable. This 'depth scale' is intended as a neutral benchmark against which any project team can

Table 5.2 A typology of relationships between different categories of actors A and B which are 'participating' or 'co-developing' with each other

	Level (−1) Denigration	Level 0 Neglect	Level 1 Learning About	Level 2 Learning From	Level 3 Learning Together	Level 4A Learning As One
Typical Processes	A makes decisions without B's involvement, (sometimes contrary to B's interests).	A makes decisions without B's involvement: ignorant or dismissive of B's interests.	A asks B's opinions, but does not feel obliged to take them into account: A makes the final decisions.	A asks B's opinions and considers B's contribution seriously. A still makes the final decisions.	Major issues are negotiated through discussion between A and B. Most decisions are made jointly, e.g. by consensus-building.	A-B consortium discusses relevant issues by focusing on the ideas themselves, rather than the source of the ideas.
Typical Attitudes	A denigrates B's ways of thinking, knowing and/or acting.	B's ways of thinking, knowing and acting are not considered.	A acknowledges that B has different ways of thinking, knowing and acting,	A recognises that there may be some value in B's ways of thinking, knowing and acting,	A recognises value in B's ways of thinking, knowing and acting, and in the added value of working with B.	No dichotomy between A and B exists; focus is on seeking mutually satisfactory solutions to shared problems.
Typical Assumptions Made by A	B's ways are inferior and possibly a threat (e.g. conceptually).	B's ways are inferior and of no real consequence or use.	B's ways are inferior, but worth noting.	B's ways may be inferior, but seem potentially useful.	A's ways and B's ways are equal in status but probably operate in different domains.	Superior ways are those that solve the problems (often co-created).
Typical Actions Taken by A	Attempt to minimize/eradicate B's ways; teach B to adopt A's own ways.	Ignore B's ways; teach B to adopt A's own ways.	Learn about B's ways, without changing own ways. May find new methods of teaching B to adopt A's own ways.	Learn from B's ways and consider making limited changes to own ways. May teach B a modified version of A's own ways.	Take into account strengths and weaknesses of both approaches. Work with B to co-create new ways at the interface between A and B ways.	Work closely with B to co-create new ways of thinking, knowing and acting in response to shared problems, drawing on all available resources.

Source: reprinted from Harder et al. (2013) 'What is Participation? Design Leads the Way to a Cross-Disciplinary Framework', Design Issues, 29(4) Autumn, p. 45.

decide its targets, according to local contexts. As noted by Hayward *et al.* (2004) there may be several reasons why less participation is appropriate in specific scenarios. Studies in other disciplines can also productively use the same levels as indicators of attitudes, approaches, assumptions, actions, or decision-making processes. We tabulate examples from several disciplines in Table 5.3 to show clear linkages across disciplines and paradigms, with the overall aim of demonstrating how levels of participation can provide a common depth scale across different settings and subjects. The typologies of participation depth illustrated here have been developed from existing action research projects across public policy, agriculture, international development, community-based health, health and social care, evaluation, environmental assessment and education.

Although some variation is inevitably appropriate, we can, with only minor adjustments, map all of them onto each other, and onto our six-category Participation Framework. Table 5.3 thus reveals the remarkable consistency in underlying understandings of participation depth across very diverse academic disciplines.

We realized, then, that our level descriptions used in intercultural education could actually be generalized for multi-disciplinary use. In the generalized sense, Level (−1) represents non-participation, where self-styled 'experts' dominate and *denigration* of stakeholders' own views might occur (Burford *et al.* 2012: 33). Level 0 represents a unidirectional flow of information from 'experts' to other stakeholders (*informing*), with no attempt to elicit their views. The generalized Level 1 represents the *acknowledgement* of other stakeholders who have potentially differing perspectives and are invited to contribute via consultation, study, or listening. However, the views of the others are unlikely to exert a substantial influence in decision-making here. Level 2 is characterized by active *engagement* with other stakeholders, whose views significantly influence and inform decision-making, although major decisions are still undertaken without them (collaboration, co-operation, or placation). Level 3 is characterized by *interaction*, meaningful exchanges of information, and shared responsibilities for planning and decision-making. Level 4 represents a scenario in which dichotomies (expert/community, researcher/respondent or designer/user) are entirely dissolved, and both partners consciously contribute knowledge and skills toward the achievement of shared common goals. This level represents *full partnership*, where all decisions are undertaken by consensus. Some authors regard the desired endpoint as a scenario in which a previously marginalized stakeholder group assumes full control of decision-making. We do not consider this scenario as an additional level of participation, but rather a new beginning. The members of the newly autonomous party can then decide what level of participation they might choose to facilitate with their partners.

This rich expansion of the 'participation depth' dimension across disciplines using our generalized levels can thus correlate terms used in other literatures and illustrates their overlapping concepts, allowing each to be identified with respect to the others in a unified context. Most importantly, it reduces the chances of any one concept being confused with another, which currently happens repeatedly;

Table 5.3 Participation typologies in contexts from different disciplines, linked by their generalized levels of participation depth

	Level (−1) Denigration	Level 0 Neglect	Level 1 Learning About	Level 2 Learning From	Level 3 Learning Together	Level 4A Learning As One
Level descriptors relating to indigenous participation in education (Harder et al. 2013).	**Denigration** indigenous knowledge (IK) explicitly denigrated in formal curricula.	**Neglect** IK not explicitly denigrated, but devalued by omission from mainstream curricula.	**Acknowledgement ('learning about')** IK described in formal curricula, usually by outsiders. Indigenous involvement in decision-making is very limited or non-existent.	**Engagement ('learning from')** Merits of IK are emphasised, but it is still seen as inferior. Limited indigenous involvement in decision-making, e.g. by boundary spanners.	**Interculturality ('learning together')** Recognition of equal status and collaborative decision-making, but dichotomy still exists.	**Full partnership ('learning as one')** Problem-based, change-oriented learning dissolves 'us and them' mindset, creating new knowledge towards shared goals. Decision-making is fully collaborative.
Level descriptors relating to resource-poor farmers' participation in agricultural research (Biggs 1989).	**Non-participation**		**Contractual participation** One social actor or stakeholder group has sole decision-making power and can be considered the owner. Others are formally or informally 'contracted' to provide services and support.	**Consultative participation** Most key decisions kept with one stakeholder group, but emphasis on consultation and gathering information from others.	**Collaborative participation** Different partners collaborate and are put on a more equal footing. Exchange of knowledge and sharing of decision-making power.	**Collegiate participation** Different actors work together as colleagues or partners. Ownership, responsibility and risk are equally distributed. Decisions made by agreement or consensus.

	No participation	Inform	Study / Listen	Take advice / Consult	Co-produce	Co-decide
Level descriptors relating to stakeholder participation in environmental assessment (Hage et al. 2010).	**No participation** No feedback, no utilization of external sources of information, no legitimisation.	**Inform** No opportunity to make a contribution: no 'real' participation.	**Study** Conduct surveys, interviews, focus groups, etc. **Listen** Set up channels for feedback / complaints.	**Take advice / Consult** Interactive workshops at key points of the project: highly goal-oriented. Can result in new perspectives.	**Co-produce** Interactive scenario development: reflective approach and use of participatory methods. Can make a major contribution to knowledge production.	**Co-decide** Joint management (e.g. of nature databases). Fulfils democratic motives.
Level descriptors relating to people's participation in development projects (Pretty 1995).	**Manipulative participation** Participation is simply a pretence.	**Passive participation** People participate by being told what has been decided.	**Participation by consultation** People answer questions but professionals are under no obligation to take on board their views. **Participation for material incentives** People provide resources, e.g. labour, in return for incentives.	**Functional participation** Groups are formed to meet predetermined objectives. Involvement may be interactive, with shared decision making, but tends to occur only after the major decisions have already been taken by external agents.	**Interactive participation** People participate in joint analysis, planning, and formation / strengthening of local institutions. Process involves interdisciplinary methodologies that seek multiple perspectives. People control local decisions.	N/A

continued

Table 5.3 Continued

	Level (–1) Denigration	Level 0 Neglect	Level 1 Learning About	Level 2 Learning From	Level 3 Learning Together	Level 4A Learning As One
Level descriptors relating to non-evaluative stakeholders' participation in evaluation (Daigneault and Jacob 2009)	**Non-participatory** Exclusive control by evaluator and/or nonparticipating evaluation sponsor.		**Limited/weak control** by participants.	**Shared control** between participants and nonparticipating evaluation sponsor.	**Substantial/strong control** by participants.	N/A
Level descriptors relating to service users' participation in health and social care research (adapted from McLaughlin 2010, citing Hanley 2004).	**Non-participation**	**Tokenism** Symbolic attempt to involve service users (to 'tick the box') or unintentional failure to establish meaningful participation.	**Consultation (I)** Views of service users are asked, but not necessarily used to influence decision making.	**Consultation (II)** Views of service users inform, and help to influence, decision making. **Collaboration (I)** Service users collaborate e.g. as members of an advisory group.	**Collaboration (II)** Service users collaborate in all/most aspects of the research process.	N/A
Level descriptors relating to community participation in community-based health research (Naylor et al. 2002).	**Non-participatory**		**Consultation** Experts present pre-determined issues; community input sought only once to 'sell' program).	**Cooperation** Community offers advice and ongoing advisory input, but decision-making rests with experts.	**Participation** Equal decision-making by experts and community.	N/A

Level descriptors relating to citizens' participation in public policy and planning (Arnstein 1969).	Manipulation	Therapy	Consultation	Placation	Partnership	N/A
	Goal of participation is to create support for decisions that have already been made, through public relations strategies.	The job is to cure or educate the participants **Informing** One-way flow of information, with no channel for feedback.	Attitude surveys, neighbourhood meetings and public enquiries. But still is just a window dressing ritual.	Co-option of hand-picked 'worthies' on to committees. Citizens can advise or plan ad infinitum, but power holders still have the right to judge legitimacy or feasibility of the advice.	Power is redistributed through negotiation between citizens and power-holders. Planning and decision-making responsibilities are shared.	

Source: reprinted from Harder et al (2013) p. 46.

reconceptualizing and redefining terms in every study becomes unnecessary, which allows cross-disciplinary scholars to build upon and develop higher-order concepts. The cross-mapping in Table 5.3 bridges the vocabulary and concepts laid out in Table 5.2, suggesting that our framework has potential for strong and consistent theory-building across disciplines. Also remarkable is that this theory-building seems possible even across paradigms, which is very encouraging for building a sound knowledge base. Note that we are not claiming any novelty in setting out such a 'Ladder of Participation' (Arnstein 1969), nor that of participation across disciplines, the aim is only to suggest some useful systemization for cross-comparison and evaluation.

As outlined above we use the term *breadth* to refer to the *diversity* of stakeholders invited to be involved in a process. Which types of stakeholders are participating? We group stakeholders in our framework so as to capture some essence of seniority and representation, as well as the numbers of people involved; for example, stakeholders include decision-makers/leaders (L), project implementers/staff managers (M), project beneficiaries/clients (C) and the wider society (W). The idea that the boundaries of such groups sometimes need to be 'spanned' by special actors means some projects use 'boundary spanners'– individuals who can relate to several groups (Hart *et al.* 2007; Wenger 1998).

Integrating depth, breadth and scope (+ output)

The previous sections clarify depth and breadth dimensions of participation. In a recent project, we realized the power of clearly setting these dimensions out against the third dimension: *scope*. Scope relates to the key stages of a project (e.g. initiation, planning, implementation, reflection, communication). Many research papers suffer from a lack of clarity about *which stage* is under discussion: the subject is under-conceptualized. Two recurring examples are that projects that are co-designed (in any sense) may not necessarily be co-initiated, and that wide participation in planning does not guarantee wide participation opportunities during implementation. Research and evaluation articles might start a discussion about participation in one stage but finish it in the context of another. Further, participation of any given stakeholder group often actually fluctuates throughout the life cycle of a project (Naylor *et al.* 2002: 1180) but specific project reports seldom clarify these changes. For all of these reasons, we have found that clearly setting out the participation landscape for every individual project, using schematics such as in Figure 5.1 can be very useful. This diagram not only compares processes within one case study (as horizontal rows) but also comparatively across case studies (the vertical axis). In a Mexican intercultural university, for example, local wise persons (*sabios locales*) participated at around Level 3–4 (Row a), while in a second case study in a Tanzanian intercultural secondary school village, herbalists were participating at Level 2 (Row c).

How, then, do these schematics enable a detailed analysis, in relation to our own project? As already outlined, the field trials described in Chapter 3 involved participatory evaluation of civil society organizations (CSOs) (see also Burford *et al.* 2013) whereby a menu of indicators was offered so that the CSOs could choose the ones with which they wished to evaluate themselves. A leader from each organization had been involved both in identifying the original need (i.e. for the evaluation in the first place, and for this type of evaluation in particular) and in overseeing the development of a menu of indicators that the groups could each choose from, depending on which ones they thought were relevant and useful. The indicators selected by each organization were allowed to be localized to modify any aspects that were deemed 'alien', and our researchers then facilitated members in developing their own assessment tools to measure each indicator, using whichever media they were comfortable with (e.g. questionnaires, theatre, painting). The main objective of the project was to produce a final assessment of the work of the organization, using the indicators it had itself chosen from the menu as most relevant, measured with its own assessment tools.

Participation in this particular case was thus possible to a Level 4 depth, with no restrictions on breadth, for each and every stage. Using a bar chart to represent participation depth, and skirts to represent the breadth of the stakeholders, we then used a different bar for each stage and arranged them in chronological order, as shown for different organizations. For each organization, a senior staff member (or leader, L) was typically involved in the initiation stage and directly helped to build the reference menu of indicators. Thus, the first bar shows a Level 4 depth (learning as one) and a narrow breadth that includes only leaders. For the planning stage, both leaders and staff customized the items they had chosen from the menu of indicators, typically being involved at Level 4, as shown in the second bar. Further breadth was achieved when the clients (i.e. children in eco-clubs) were asked for input on the localization of the indicators, achieving Level 2.

The third bar in each case study row in Figure 5.1 shows the implementation stage, where all staff members and clients were typically quite deeply involved in developing and using assessment tools with which they were comfortable to actually measure the indicators they had agreed on. The second row (b) shows the results of a particularly interesting case already mentioned: the use of a 'hand painting circle', in which the young participants were each asked to paint something on their neighbour's hand that reflected their feelings after a reforestation campaign. Words used to describe the paintings were recorded as examples of emotional vocabulary associated with the campaign, allowing a qualitative understanding of its affective impact on the youth. This 'learning as one' with the researchers achieved a participation depth score of Level 4 for that particular project.

Most of the organizations had moderate scores in the reflection and communication stages because they were not priority stages in this study; however, the organization represented in this second row (b) produced deep reflection from leaders, staff, and clients, and it used the measurements generated to communicate in an articulate way to its donors and other organizations about the worth of its work. The results described can be contrasted with those of a third

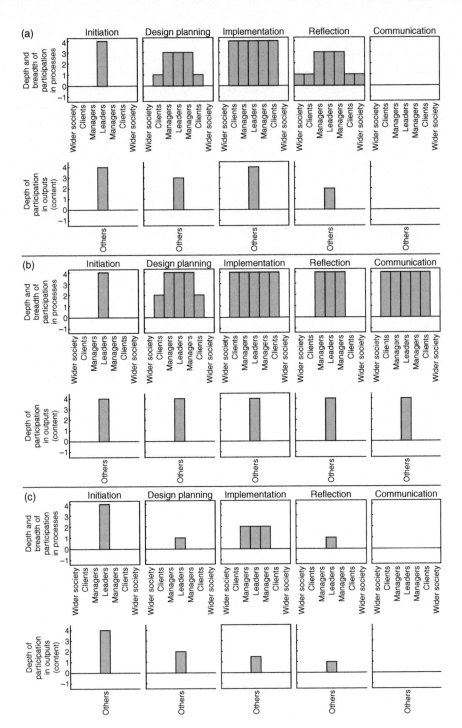

Figure 5.1 Schematics showing integrated analysis of depth, breadth and scope of specific participatory projects by the ESDinds team.

Source: reprinted from Harder *et al.* (2013: 49).

organization, in which only leaders were involved in the initiation, design planning, and reflection stages, and only few staff were involved (via written questionnaires) in the implementation stage, scoring a depth of Level 1 as illustrated in the third row (c) of this diagram.

All together, the schematics in Figure 5.1 allow clear visualization and communication of participation activities in several dimensions, facilitating cleaner analysis, reflection, and exploration of the related topics. Without such a schematic, reflection remains murky, analysis difficult and communication hampered. With or without the schematics, we propose that this 3-D participation framework provides a basis for clear conversations. In our case, this process valuably illuminated some of the differences in outcomes across different groups in our field trials; and suggested that for our particular project, it was critical to have equitable and *deep* participation in the process. However, at the same time, undertaking this work enabled us to set yet another dimension that is also useful, that of output content.

In the previous sections we have discussed the characteristics of participation, but not its effect – the processes, but not the outputs. In our example, the main objective was to obtain evaluation measurements of each organization's performance – in its own terms and in self-determined domains. Such results were not achievable by the researchers alone because they had insufficient understanding of the organization's context. Neither was it achievable by any organization's leaders alone because they had insufficient understanding of evaluation methods. Thus, the quality of the *overall output* for this particular work actually depended critically on the depth of the partnership, and evidence of such collaboration could be sought in the content of the output from the implementation stage. For our three sample case study rows, then, we have added a set of outputs charts beneath each. To better understand participation concepts overall, the outputs from all stages are also shown in this example. For other studies, and in other disciplines, other output types (or none) might be important, but the same framework and schematics can be used.

What would this new dimension, 'evidence of participation' in the output content, actually look like? At Level 1 or 2, the content would predictably contain contributions primarily from the higher-powered partner. At Level 4, full, appropriate contributions from both partners would present, and possibly would no longer be separable. In our example, the indicators (and related measurements) were creations that were not obtainable from either partner alone, nor could they be 'broken down' into components, contributed by parts from each: They were thus deemed Level 4. In other studies, a different output might be the priority. If co-creation were key, then the initiation stage might be expected to produce an output (e.g. the target product) showing evidence of Level 3 or Level 4 participation content. For community engagement projects, the final plans coming out of the planning stage might be the most crucial and might be expected to show Levels 3 to 4. In user-centred design, user feedback in the reflection stage would probably be the most significant, and participation in earlier stages almost irrelevant. Thus, although the schematic is generally applicable, different components are critical in different work. Other aspects of output have not been presented here, such as stimulation of secondary participation, but could easily be incorporated.

In conclusion: we have suggested in this chapter that by laying out participation concepts by depth and breadth at each stage separately, the clear, detailed visualization allows higher-level conceptualization, not just in our own work but in any work concerned with participation. The clarity it provides enables more accuracy in recognising what kinds of participation are taking place, and in analysing the impacts. We also hope to use it to stimulate clearer discussions about more complex design concepts, such as sustainable design and spiral dynamics (Beck and Cowan 2005), which we think could lead to parallel advances in other disciplines where participation is a current topic.

Using generalizable schematics such as these can thus enable scholars and practitioners across diverse fields to more easily and quickly place each other's conversations without confusion, and thus move toward deeper understandings and a linked body of knowledge. We hope work like this will catalyze step-wise advances toward a sound knowledge base for participation across disciplines. And whilst we have clarified some details regarding the depth, breadth, and scope of participation in a manner useful to a variety of disciplines, this chapter has left open a discussion on the *purposes* that participation can have in different contexts.

Whilst we will touch on this in the conclusion of this book, there is still much to explore around paradigmatic differences and paradigm crossings, across diverse disciplines including that framed as research through design.

Notes

1 See, for example, Alastair Fuad-Luke, *Design Activism: Beautiful Strangeness for a Sustainable World* (London: Earthscan 2009); John R. Ehrenfeld, *Sustainability by Design: A Subversive Strategy for Transforming Our Consumer Culture* (New Haven: Yale University Press, 2008); Elizabeth Sanders, 'Design Research in 2006', *Design Research Quarterly* 1 (2006): 1–8; Stuart Walker, *Sustainable by Design: Explorations in Theory and Practice* (London: Earthscan, 2006); Yanki Lee, 'Design Participation Tactics: The Challenges and New Roles for Designers in the Co-Design Process', *CoDesign: International Journal of CoCreation in Design and the Arts* 4 (2008): 31–50; Thomas Binder, Eva Brandt, and Judith Gregory, 'Design Participation(-s)', *CoDesign: International Journal of CoCreation in Design and the Arts* 4 (2008): 1–3; and Joan Greenbaum and Daria Loi, 'Participation, the Camel and the Elephant of Design: An Introduction', *CoDesign: International Journal of CoCreation in Design and the Arts* 8 (2012): 81–85.
2 The exact category boundaries are not critical here, but worked productively for us. The five stages of design thinking of Tim Brown (2008), for example, could be used instead.

References

Amo, C. and Cousins, J. B. (2007) 'Going Through the Process: An Examination of the Operationalization of Process Use in Empirical Research on Evaluation', *New Directions for Evaluation*, (116), pp. 5–26.

Arnstein, S. R. (1969) 'A Ladder of Participation', *American Institute of Planners Journal*, 35, pp. 216–224.

Beck, D. E. and Cowan, C. (2005) *Spiral Dynamics: Mastering Values. Leadership and Change*. Chichester: Wiley-Blackwell.

Bell, S., Morse, S., and Shah, R. A. (2012) 'Understanding Stakeholder Participation in Research as Part of Sustainable Development', *Journal of Environmental Management*, 101, pp. 13–22.

Brown, T. (2008) 'Design Thinking', *Harvard Business Review*, 86(6), pp. 84–92.

Burford, G., Kissmann, S., Rosado-May, F. J., Alvarado Dzul, S. H., and Harder, M. K. (2012) 'Indigenous Participation in Intercultural Education: Learning from Mexico and Tanzania', *Ecology and Society*, 17, p. 33.

Burford, G., Velasco, I., Janouskova, S., Zahradnik, M., Hak, T., Podger, D., Piggot, G., and Harder, M. K. (2013) 'Field Trials of a Novel Toolkit for Evaluating "Intangible" Values-Related Dimensions of Projects', *Evaluation and Program Planning*, 36, pp. 1–14. Retrieved from www.sciencedirect.com/science/article/pii/S0149718912000444.

Cornwall, A. and Jewkes, R. (1995) 'What Is Participatory Research?' *Social Science and Medicine*, 41, pp. 1667–1676.

Cousins, J. B. (2007) 'Process Use in Theory, Research and Practice', *New Directions for Evaluation*, p. 116.

Cousins, J. B., Donohue, J. J., and Bloom, G. A. (1996) 'Collaborative Evaluation in North America: Evaluators' Self-Reported Opinions, Practices and Consequences', *Evaluation Practice*, 17, pp. 207–226.

Cox, T., Karanika, M., Griffiths, A., and Houdmont, J., (2007) 'Evaluating Organizational-Level Work Stress Interventions: Beyond Traditional Methods', *Work & Stress*, 21(4), pp. 348–362.

Crishna, B. (2007) 'Participatory Evaluation (I) – Sharing Lessons from Fieldwork in Asia', *Child: Care Health and Development*, 33, pp. 217–223.

Daigneault, P.-M., and Jacob, S. (2009) 'Toward Accurate Measurement of Participation: Rethinking the Conceptualization and Operationalization of Participatory Evaluation', *American Journal of Evaluation*, 30, pp. 330–348.

Forss, K., Rebien, C., and Carlsson, J. (2002) 'Process Use of Evaluations: Types of Use that Precede Lessons Learned and Feedback', *Evaluation*, 8(1), pp. 29–45.

Guijt, I., and Kaul Shah, M. (1998) *The Myth of Community: Gender Issues in Participatory Development*. London: Intermediate Technology Publications.

Harder, M. K., Burford, G., and Hoover, E. (2013) 'What Is Participation? Design Leads the Way to a Cross-Disciplinary Framework', *DesignIssues*, 29(4) Autumn.

Hart, R. A. (1992) *Children's Participation: From Tokenism to Citizenship*. Florence: UNICEF and International Child Development Centre.

Hart, A., Maddison, E., and Wolff, D. (Eds.) (2007) 'Introduction', in *Community-University Partnerships in Practice*. Leicester, UK: National Institute of Adult Continuing Education.

Hayward, C., Simpson, L., and Wood, L. (2004) 'Still Left Out in the Cold: Problematising Participatory Research and Development', *Sociologia Ruralis*, 44, 95–108.

Jacob, S., Ouvrard, L., and Belanger, J. F. (2011) 'Participatory Evaluation and Process Use Within a Social Aid Organization for At-Risk Families and Youth', *Evaluation and Program Planning*, 34(2), pp. 113–123.

Naylor, P.-J., Wharf-Higgin, J., Blair, L., Green, L. W., and O'Connor, B (2002) 'Evaluating the Participatory Process in a Community-Based Heart Health Project', *Social Science and Medicine*, 55, pp. 1173–1187.

Pretty, J.N., Guijt, I., Thompson, J., and Scoones, I. (1995) *Participatory Learning and Action: A Trainer's Guide*. London: IIED.

Ruitenbeek, J. and Cartier, C. (2001) *The Invisible Wand: Adaptive Co-Management as an Emergent Strategy in Complex Bio-Economic Systems*. Jakarta: Center for International Forestry Research.

Springett, J. (2003) 'Issues in Participatory Evaluation'. In Minkler, M. and Wallerstein, N. (Eds.) *Community-Based Participatory Research for Health*. San Francisco, CA: Jossey-Bass.

Wenger, E. (1998) *Communities of Practice: Learning, Meaning and Identity*. Cambridge, UK: Cambridge University Press.

6 Values and validity

The embryonic origins of the co-research set out in this book started with concerns about values and validity: *why* did funders have the right to assess projects only according to their own values, and *what could be done* to make tangible the less formalized values of civil society organizations (CSOs)? The previous chapters have often raised issues about what gives validity to a values-based framework, centred on making explicit intangible shared group values. Validity is vital; one of the 'wicked' problems (Rittel and Webber 1973) about discussing and using values concepts and indicators has always been that these seem non-measurable; at best relative and at worst, uniquely personal. Yet we have maintained throughout that the most important aspect of our research must be that the resultant values indicators be considered valid by our central actors, that is, the CSO groups. They must be considered by them to be relevant for the purpose intended: to represent core CSO values-in-action and to be capable of producing recognizable measures of related achievements. This kind of measurement validity – an all-encompassing, overall validity running true through concepts, operationalization, measures, interpretation and then usage – is denoted as unitary validity (Messick 1995). Because it is so difficult to achieve and generally to deal with, many researchers instead pick out what they deem to be the most critical elemental aspects of unitary validity in their areas, and scrutinize those. Thus, many academics may focus on sampling validity for measures to be used by scientists, and on construct validity for measures for use by theorists.

In this chapter, we want to explore in more depth how unitary validity was embedded and became inherent in our values-based framework system. We also explore how 'deep' participatory processes seem to underpin many aspects of that unitary validity. A previous chapter, for example, outlined our framework's propensity to produce item validity – where a valid connection can be made between chosen measurements and what is being measured. In this chapter, we wish to systematically consider each element of validity that makes up unitary validity, and see how our action co-research through design has influenced their nature.

Academic frameworks and models are typically built incrementally with links to existing systems of knowledge, including definitions and boundaries for concepts, propositions and theories. In these cases, researchers must consider with each new construction whether they have preserved existing validities associated with those elements. Conversely, when we use an emergent values-based approach, local validity arguments must be constructed with internal consistency, and only later tested against formal (propositional) knowledge and its validity.

Because of our central guiding principle that our final framework must have unitary validity – that is, that the use of any resulting measures are considered valid for the pre-agreed purpose of CSO self-evaluation – it was necessary to introduce localization. And at the same time as generating a remarkably high – perhaps unprecedented – level of unitary validity from the perspective of the organization concerned, localization introduces a great deal of complexity into any attempt to relate local evaluation measures to external measures or theories, or to compare them between organizations. At this stage we do not claim to achieve these particular aspects of valid generalizability or transferability. Instead we will first scrutinize the resulting levels of the remaining major area of validity – content validity: the extent to which items on an instrument represent the content being measured. How could we be sure that the pool of trigger statements (proto-indicators) captures and is actually measuring the completeness of individual and group constructs (articulated through shared value-labels) in different contexts? How can we check that we are not just measuring one dimension of a multi-faceted understanding of a particular value? Here we follow Onwuegbuzie *et al.* (2007), whose work aimed to develop a meta-validation model, extending Messick, and using mixed method research techniques. We therefore characterize content-related validity as comprised of three aspects: (1) face validity; (2) item validity; and (3) sampling validity. It should be noted that discussions of validity are rife with multiple terminologies; we will aim to make increasingly clear our understanding of these aspects as the chapter progresses. Here we start from the following simple definitions:

- Face validity: whether the test appears (at face value) to measure what it claims to, as rated by the people who take the test.
- Item validity: the extent to which an individual item measures what it purports to measure.
- Sampling validity: how well test measures cover all the areas we wanted them to cover.

Exploring our content validity

Our approach has co-developed an apparently new framework for understanding human values, their operationalization and their measurement in the context of group shared values. As already outlined in previous chapters, values, from this perspective, can neither be objectively neutral or universally 'true' independent of context, nor do they relate only to the subjective emotional states of individuals. It is their 'inter-subjective objectivity' (Colvert 2007) that matters, that is, how they come to be shared. Values may thus be regarded as categories that are *assigned to* behaviour and attitudes through subjective, personal acts of inter-pretation, rather than as concrete, mutually independent entities. Through a process of dialogue in which different people share and compare their individual perspectives, collective – or, more precisely, inter-subjective – understandings of values can be achieved. How, then, are face, item and sampling validity criteria met in this kind of framework? Using the Echeri case study as an example, each of these will be explored in turn.

In order to do this systematically, we have separated our values framework process into three stages: assigning indicators to values; assigning assessment tools to indicators; and assigning value meanings to the assessment data. This is outlined in more detail in Table 6.1.

Face validity

As already noted, face validity is described here as the extent to which the respondents regard the items on an instrument as relevant, important and inter-esting (Onwuegbuzie *et al.* 2007) and has elsewhere been defined as 'member checks' by a sub-sample of respondents (Lather 1986; Guba and Lincoln 1989). Reason and Rowan (1981) explain that face validity can be increased by taking tentative results back to the research subject, and refining them in the light of the subject's reactions. For face validity, value domains thus need to be clearly and explicitly defined in an inter-subjective way, using indicators that are rel-evant, important and interesting to the participating group. As outlined in Chapter 3, for Echeri the value 'unity in diversity' had been understood and confirmed as important by all partner CSOs in the consortium, and for one of them it constituted a core value. During the field-testing, however, some Echeri staff members objected to the use of the term 'unity' in this value. It was felt to be associated, in their sphere of work, with uniformity or imposition, and also to be too abstract for their youth group participants to understand. At the same time, every single indicator within this category was considered locally relevant to the work of Echeri and selected for application. These indicators were viewed by the CSO staff as a coherent set expressing a common value concept – the same one as 'unity in diversity', but amended in a focus group discussion with the youth to *colaboración en diversidad* (which can be translated into English as 'collaboration in diversity'), effectively a synonym. This 'unity in diversity' example illustrates that what is most crucial in defining a value domain is not the term itself, but the underlying concepts framing it. Thus, people using the same values vocabulary may in fact have differing and even conflicting value constructs in mind; while people objecting strongly to a given value term might in fact be in favour of the underlying construct, and simply refer to it differently. This means (in common with theoretically derived approaches to measuring values) that in order for a given value to be meaningfully measured it is critical not merely to name, but to explicitly articulate the frame that turns the value label into a clearly delineated construct – ideally *before* seeing the pre-defined

Table 6.1 Sample criteria for demonstrating different types of content-related validity during the three interpretive stages of a values-based evaluation

Interpretive process	Criteria for content-related validity		
	Face validity	Item validity	Sampling validity
Assigning indicators to values (V→I)	Value domains are clearly and explicitly defined in an inter-subjective way, using indicators that are relevant, important and interesting to the CSO.	Every individual indicator fits (according to the CSO's internal consensus) within the value domain(s) to which it has been assigned.	All the indicators assigned to a given value, taken together, fully cover the CSO's inter-subjective definition of that value domain: no locally important aspect of the value has been missed.
Assigning assessment tools to indicators (I→AT)	Indicator domains are clearly and explicitly defined in an inter-subjective way, using context-appropriate assessment methods and specific components of assessment tools (e.g. questions) that are relevant, important and interesting to the CSO.	Every component of every assessment tool fits (according to the CSO's internal consensus) within the indicator domain(s) to which it has been assigned.	All the assessment tools for a given indicator, taken together, fully cover the CSO's inter-subjective understanding of that indicator domain: no locally important aspect of the indicator has been missed.
Assigning value meanings to data (D→V)	Research participants 'recognize themselves' in the final interpretation of the data, i.e. the values-related conclusions are both plausible and interesting within the CSO's local context.	Each of the separate results generated by the assessment tools can be related back to the value(s) being measured, i.e. the data have not stepped outside the value domain(s).	All the data generated by the assessment tools, taken together, approximate a 'measurement' of the value (as it was defined inter-subjectively by the CSO).

indicators. In the Echeri case, this was achieved by the nature of the focus group discussion. The youth were asked to provide their own definitions and real-life examples for four of the six different values, and then, with the project director, to explore the commonalities and differences by drawing lines horizontally, vertically, diagonally and in a spiral fashion between them (as described in Chapter 3). While the details may differ from one CSO to another, this suggested that some kind of systematic construct-definition process is essential for establishing both face and content-related validity.

The way in which Echeri's co-evaluators handled the value of 'care and respect for the community of life' provides an interesting contrast to the above example. In this case, the value term was recognized and accepted enthusiastically by the youth group members as well as Echeri staff – perhaps because of their own connection to the Earth Charter Initiative, which had proposed the term to the original EU-funded consortium. Nonetheless, the operational definition of this value that Echeri staff chose to adopt was a relatively narrow one. Of the 79 indicators that had been connected to it by the original consortium, only ten were selected by Echeri as being of relevance in the specific context of evaluating the Juatarhu youth group and the school-based workshops. Many aspects that the consortium had initially included in its own definition, such as pro-environmental behaviours (sustainable waste management, control of carbon emissions, recycling, etc.) and interpersonal manifestations of care and respect, were thus excluded from Echeri's local definition of the same value. This underpinned the centrality of *face* validity to our process; that the value indicators appeared effective and relevant to the group themselves.

Item validity

Item validity requires that every individual indicator fits (according to the CSO's internal consensus) within the value domain(s) to which it has been assigned. Did an individual indicator measure what it was intended to measure, in relation to a core value for Echeri? A revelation that startled the researchers was that indicators that had been derived from six specific values, and were initially assumed to have a one-to-one correspondence with them, were being assigned to entirely *different* values by CSO representatives in the field. In many cases, these were values that the CSOs themselves would describe as central to their mission, but they appeared less related to the six named values that the original consortium had initially set out to operationalize. Here, as previously outlined, it is inter-subjective objectivity that provides the key to interpretation. An individual indicator such as 'people feel that they are encouraged to express their opinions' may be described by one group of co-evaluators as having item validity for the measurement of empowerment; by a second as representing respect and care; and by a third as simultaneously indicating openness and participation. There is no cosmically objective truth stating that this item is invariably valid for measuring some particular value – indeed, we would argue that there may be *no* concrete values with an objectively verifiable existence. What matters is only group consensus – the ability of a CSO director to tell donors, for example that 'we are all agreed that this is an indicator of empowerment in our own project'. In this sense, every short-list of indicators has inherent item validity, provided that the participatory process used to generate it is an adequate one.

To conclude the discussion of assigning indicators to values, it is important to highlight the fact that the wording of the individual indicators is indicative rather than fixed. Rather, CSOs are strongly encouraged to translate them into their own internal language, effectively using them as templates for the construction of their own customized, locally appropriate indicators, and thereby to maximise the face validity of their evaluation. This may be as simple a process as replacing the word 'people' with 'youth' or 'staff', or 'entity' with 'school', or it may entail adding new words or even entire phrases to the indicators.

Sampling validity

For sampling validity, the aim is that all the indicators assigned to a given value, taken together, fully cover the CSO's inter-subjective definition of that value domain: no locally important aspect of the value has been missed. If Echeri staff had complained that something was missing – that the available indicators did not adequately encompass their own understanding of each of the concepts – the project framework would have failed to have stable and consistent results, unless new indicators were invented to fill the gap (which in turn could undermine the generalizability of the approach). In reality, when Echeri's founding director was explicitly asked whether she felt that any indicators were missing, she responded in the negative and said that she was satisfied that the value had been fully covered.

In our values-based approach, item validity and sampling validity at the first (assigning values to indicators) stage both depend on face validity, in that the co-evaluators define value domains pragmatically according to their own perceptions and priorities. CSO staff can thus declare that individual indicators relate to a given value *as they have defined it themselves*, rather than according to its theoretical definition in academic literature; and that the total set of indicators samples whichever manifestation(s) of the value they regard as important, rather than attempting to measure the totality of a theoretical construct. Provided that there is genuine stakeholder participation, item validity is thus intrinsic to the participation process. Sampling validity, by contrast, is not inherent, as it would be possible for a group to conclude that the available indicators do not fully cover its consensus definition of a certain value and that something important is missing. In this case, the group would be faced with the choice of inventing new indicators to fill the gap, or proceeding with the analysis anyway while acknowledging the deficiencies of the model.

Assigning assessment tools to indicators

The above has outlined the criteria for content-related validity across face, item and sampling validity during the first stage of our process, that is, assigning indicators to values. What then, are the criteria that must be fulfilled in order for content validity to be maintained in the next part of the process – from the interpretation to the assessment stage; that is, where particular assessment tools are linked to the value indicators? We found that there were two. The first of these is the local appropriateness of the overall method that is used, and the second is the extent to which the individual items that make up assessment tools – such as specific questions in a questionnaire, survey or interview schedule – are relevant, important and interesting to the CSO. Both of these are determined through consensus.

As previously noted, the Echeri case study also exemplifies methodological localization, where the specificities of the context helped generate the process. This might be termed an 'intercultural' approach to research methodology. Unlike multiculturalism, which can tend to preserve parallel cultural heritages, interculturalism 'acknowledges and enables cultures to have currency, to be exchanged, to circulate, to be modified and evolve' (Powell and Sze 2004). This aligns with research through design, as a means of creating new knowledges. As Cantle (2012: 212) writes:

> Interculturalism is about changing mindsets by creating new opportunities across cultures to support intercultural activity and it's about thinking, planning and acting interculturally. Perhaps, more importantly still, it is about envisioning the world as we want it to be, rather than be determined by our separate past histories.

As already outlined, for example, recognizing the variable literacy levels of participants in the Echeri programmes, the co-evaluators designed assessments that would engage children and youth in a similar way to Echeri's pedagogical activities, which are mainly creative, non-cognitive and based on the arts and physical movement. As well as the spatial and corporeal surveys, and hand-painting activity described in Chapter 3, these also included framing comprehension exercises in terms of role-play, rather than written tests. To increase face validity still further, the spatial survey was linked to a powerful local symbol, the spiral, which represents several different concepts in the indigenous culture and is used in many of Echeri's activities. These modified methodologies were very enthusiastically received by the youth, to the extent that they later replicated them independently during a national youth camp, thus confirming the researchers' assumption of high face validity.

We would suggest that in the assignation of assessment tools to an indicator, as well as the assignation of indicators to a value, item validity is intrinsic. Only those assessment tools that 'fit' into the indicator domain, as it has been inter-subjectively defined within the CSO, will be used in practice. In terms of sampling validity, too, the argument that we articulated above for the earlier stages remains true: that is, there is no expectation that the assessment tools will constitute a fully comprehensive operationalization of the indicator, acknowledging every possible nuance of meaning. Rather, what is sought is a measurement or combination of measurements that encompasses the indicator's consensually defined meaning(s) *within the specific context,* with the caveat that triangulation is needed – not only between qualitative and quantitative methods, but also between discourse and observed behaviour – to check that that the measures do indeed test what they purport to test (this is covered in more detail below).

Assigning value-related meanings to assessment data

The final stage of our process is the assignment of value-related meanings to assessment data. In order to be sure that content-related validity has been maintained throughout the values-based process, it is necessary to make a logical link between the data generated by the assessment tools, and the original inter-subjective interpretation of the value. This stage also provides a useful cross-check of the content-related validity of the preceding stages. If content-related validity is high at both of the two initial stages, it should follow that it will also be high at the third and final stage. If, however, anything has been missed out or incorrectly assigned during the initial stages, it will be clearly highlighted at this final stage of generating value-related meanings from the data collected:

- If, for example, the assessment tools are generating results that cannot be related logically to the value(s) that co-evaluators set out to measure, this could suggest either (1) that one or more 'mistakes' were made in the initial assignation of indicators to the value(s), according to their inter-subjective definitions; or (2) that the assigned assessment tools were not really appropriate for measuring those indicators.
- Similarly, if the group consensus is that the value has not been adequately 'measured' because something important has been missed out, this could imply either (1) that new indicators would be required for a full measurement; or that (2) some important assessment tools have been omitted for particular indicators.

Face validity, at this final stage, is associated with self-recognition: whether the conclusions drawn from the data are not only interesting and relevant, but also plausible to the CSO, i.e. whether participants can 'see their faces' in the values-related findings. In the Echeri example, the data gathered from post-evaluation interviews provided strong evidence that this was the case. We would argue that, provided that there is a strong and deep participatory process throughout the evaluation (see the previous chapter) and that the previous stages have been carried out with adequate face validity as discussed above, we would not expect the third and final step to be problematic in this respect.

Framework implementation and construct-validity

The discussion of validity so far in this chapter has concentrated on the 'internal' structure, that is, the way in which indicators, values, assessment instruments and analysis are connected. However, we also need to consider the validity of the overall framework itself, in the procedures through which it is implemented. Any analytical framework is itself 'constructed'; that is based on a simplifying abstraction by the researchers, in order to both conceptualise the problem, and to have a doable means of investigating it. This is called construct-related validity, namely 'the evidential basis for score interpretation' (Messick 1995) or 'the extent to which an instrument can be interpreted as a meaningful measure of some characteristic or quality' (Onwuegbuzie *et al.* 2007). This translates, in the context of our evaluation process, into two distinct questions. The first of these can be framed as: 'do we have sufficient evidence to interpret the data generated by these assessment tools as a meaningful measure of this indicator?' Whenever this is demonstrated to be true for every one of the indicators that have been (or can be) inter-subjectively assigned to a given value, the second question can be asked as follows: 'do we have sufficient evidence to interpret the pooled data relating to all of these indicators as a meaningful measure of this value?'

Content-related validity, as explained above, is necessary but not sufficient in itself for these two questions to be answered in the affirmative. In order for the final data to be interpretable as a meaningful measure of a value within a specific CSO, the minimum requirements would be to ensure that, according to that CSO's own group consensus, (1) the value and indicator domains had been clearly and explicitly defined; (2) the indicators fitted into the value domain, and the assessment tools into their respective indicator domains; and (3) no critically important aspects had been omitted, whether at the level of values or of individual indicators. Yet, as Messick (1995) has emphasized, validity is not a property of the test or assessment as such, but rather of the *meaning of the test scores*. This, in turn, depends on the people responding, and the specific context in which the assessment is taking place. This point is further clarified by distinguishing between content-related validity as 'logically based' and construct-related validity as 'empirically based' (Onwuegbuzie *et al.* 2007). Thus, even after designing a theoretically sound assessment system for measuring a value within a CSO, and demonstrating that every indicator and every assessment tool is consistent with the system's internal logic, it would still be possible to render the final conclusions invalid by *implementing* that system in a biased way. We can never claim, then, to have developed a universally valid system for measuring human values, but only a system that has the potential to yield valid results under appropriate test conditions.

What, then, are these appropriate conditions? The key issues here are first about possible biases in the system – where participants' responses and researchers' measurements may be affected by the ways questions are asked and answered – and second about the extent to which different assessment measures can be shown to correlate with each other. These could undermine the face validity, which underpins the whole enterprise. Each of these two questions will next be looked at in turn.

Validity and potential bias

Messick (1995) highlights the importance of evaluating the intended and unintended consequences of score interpretation and use, whether positive or negative. This can occur when aspects of the task are either unduly difficult or unduly easy for certain individuals or groups. This can be a major source of bias in test scoring and interpretation. For example, when tests of subject matter knowledge are based on reading comprehension, this unfairly disadvantages individuals with poor literacy skills or limited English proficiency. The participatory nature of our values-based approach deliberately provides opportunities for such issues to be identified and addressed: as already described, the non-verbal assessment methods used at Echeri, for example, were developed in response to the early realization that low participant literacy levels would render written questionnaires inappropriate.

Another potential source of bias is called social desirability response bias (SDRB) – described as a tendency to present oneself favourably, or to obtain approval by responding in a culturally and socially acceptable manner (Crowne and Marlowe 1960). Thus, SDRB may entail either over-reporting activities that are deemed to be socially or culturally desirable, or under-reporting those deemed undesirable. Fisher and Katz (2000) explain this as follows: since values are a conception of what is desirable within a culture, associations between measures of SDRB and self-reported values are entirely to be expected, as both have a desirability component. This suggests that most ethics-based studies will suffer from SDRB, and need to take this into account, to make sure that research is still valid.

Fisher and Katz suggest several strategies that can be used to reduce SDRB in sensitive variables. One that is particularly relevant at our second stage of linking indicators to assessment methods is question wording (see also Orne 1969). The extent of SDRB, and hence the validity of results, could easily be influenced by the specific ways in which individual indicators are converted into questions for surveys or interviews. Jo (2000) has observed that respondents find it easier to express their opinions on sensitive issues in indirect and impersonal ways than in direct personal ways, and hence that an effective way of controlling SDRB is to ask respondents about what *other people* think about sensitive issues, rather than what they themselves think.

Another strategy for reducing SDRB is increasing response anonymity (Fisher 1993). Written survey questionnaires can be a very useful method of collecting data anonymously, but anonymity poses a real challenge when working with less literate populations. It could be increased, for example, through confidential interviews conducted by an external researcher, or 'secret ballot' surveys in which respondents use, for example, ballot papers of different colours. We would suggest that if a particular indicator is both highly sensitive and critically important to an organization, it may be important to pre-test assessment tools to optimize question wordings for SDRB reduction before using them with a large population.

Increasing validity through triangulation

As with evaluation in general, overall validity is greatly enhanced by triangulation of data, that is, by using mixed modes assessment methods. Lather (1986) clarifies that this term does not refer only to multiple measures, but also to multiple data sources, methods and theoretical schemes. Thus, measuring an individual value indicator in a rigorous way demands two or (preferably) more distinct methods of data collection, ideally combining qualitative and quantitative methods for weakness minimization (Onwuegbuzie *et al.* 2007). In the Echeri case study, for example, the combination of the spatial survey and focus group generated a much richer understanding of the dynamics of the Juatarhu youth group than either of these methods could have achieved in isolation. It should be noted that the research conducted at Echeri was a pilot and developmental rather than a 'model' case study. In particular, relying exclusively on discourse to measure values-based indicators is always potentially problematic, because of the already noted likely influence of SDRB on research dealing with 'ethical' or 'moral' issues. It is crucial, therefore, to supplement the findings from discourse-based assessment tools, such as surveys and focus groups, with observations of real behaviour wherever possible. This was approximated at Echeri, due to time limitations, by observing the state of tree nurseries in the different schools. In other initial field visits, structured assessment sheets were designed to help non-participant observers to make systematic records of specific behaviours during the course of regular project activities, such as 'interrupting others' or 'remaining silent during group discussions'.

In addition, we developed three key criteria that were centred on reducing any researcher bias in analysing data, so as to support the validity of the value and indicator constructs derived from the research. These were confirmability, credibility and transferability.

- **Confirmability:** given that the coding of qualitative data is an interpretive labour, the team of six researchers established a common coding vocabulary, reviewed one another's coding, and critiqued and confirmed one another's findings and interpretations. This enabled them to avoid, as far as possible, bias, unwarranted inferences or unclear or impractical conceptualizations. This meant that the preliminary constructs in terms of values and indicators had a great deal of confirmability, held by Lincoln and Guba (1985) to be the qualitative equivalent of the criterion of objectivity in quantitative research.
- **Credibility:** An extension of confirmability, this refers not only to the internal consistency, bias reduction and rigour of the researchers' constructs,

but also to their fidelity to the research participants' own perspective. If the set of values that the researchers ascribed to the CSOs, and the indicators elicited from them, were not recognized by those same participants as theirs, they would not be described as credible, however confirmable the research-ers' interpretations might be. The values definitions and associated indi-cators were thus subjected to 'member checks', as a sample of participants from each contributing CSO reviewed the researchers' construction of their values and associated indicators, and offered confirmation, amendment or critique. Credibility, in the Lincoln and Guba (1985) model, plays the function in qualitative research that 'internal validity' does in quantitative research.

- **Transferability:** The aim of this final phase of the research was not merely to find out what each of the participating CSOs considered its values to be, and how they might be indicated in practice; rather, it was to create a set of values-based indicators for field testing in new organizations. It was thus critical that the final selection of values and indicators were considered rel-evant by all four partner CSOs, thus achieving transferability, described by Lincoln and Guba (1985) as the functional equivalent of 'external validity' associated with quantitative research. A preliminary measure of transfer-ability was ensured by the process of collective prioritisation, selection and confirmation, by all CSO partners, of the values and indicators extracted from individual CSO data. The CSOs that participated in the ESDinds EU-funded phase of the research were also sampled for diversity, in order to maximise transferability.

Conclusion: towards a different kind of validity

An important concern about validity – especially with our emphasis on the cen-trality of unitary validity – is about the extent to which the framework offered here can be extended beyond its effectiveness for specific groups. Generalizabil-ity relates to the extent to which meanings and use associated with a set of scores can be generalized to other populations (Onwuegbuzie *et al.* 2007). It has been further elucidated by Messick (1995) as setting the boundaries of score meaning, while also encompassing traditional reliability concerns such as elim-inating measurement errors attributable to the sampling of tasks, occasions and scorers. However, we would argue that in some respects, the concept of general-izability is not merely irrelevant but antithetical to the principle of inter-subjective objectivity at the heart of this values-based approach. The very nature of the project evaluation demonstrated here is that it reflects the CSO's own priorities in its current circumstances: both indicators and assessment tools are localizable, so by definition they are neither generalized nor generalizable. We hypothesize that the evaluation priorities of most CSOs are dynamic rather than static: the achievement (or acknowledged non-achievement) of the ori-ginal project objectives results in new conceptions of what is 'important', which of the important constructs within a project can be taken for granted, and which ones require measurement. Even if the conceptualisation of the constructs requiring measurement remains relatively static, the *reasons* for measuring them may evolve from one year to the next. It is, in principle, unlikely that the same organization would wish to measure identical indicators in identical ways at different times.

The situation is radically changed, however, if monitoring and evaluation systems based on value-indicators are imposed by donors or other external agencies, rather than being co-designed by CSOs and researchers. It could easily be imagined that a donor would request an organization to repeat exactly the same evaluation procedures year after year, regardless of changes in the CSO's own priorities and understandings, in the hope of being able to 'quantify' project impact by comparing successive measurements. In these circumstances, it is reasonable to raise issues of generalizability, but they would have to be considered on a case-by-case basis.

The project, then, both meets key validity claims, and is critical of the conventional frameworks through which validity has often constructed and then assumed. As Habermas (1972) highlights, the traditional concepts of validity in research – as discussed here – are grounded mainly in the positivistic tradition. Yet for post-positivistic action research, concerned with effecting change in society, the question of validity takes on new dimensions. In particular, a crucial question is whether the research meets its goal of generating transformative or empowering outcomes, which has been referred to as 'catalytic validity' (Lather 1986; see also Habermas 1972). In contrast to positivistic validity types, aimed at exploring the validity of the conclusions that can be drawn at the end of a specific research process, catalytic validity goes a step further by questioning the validity of the process itself. Thus, emancipatory action research is 'validated' not only by collecting evidence to show that it has measured what it was intended to measure, but also by demonstrating that it has achieved what it was intended to achieve. If social change was an explicit goal, but no change has been accomplished, then in a crucial sense the research can be described as lacking validity.

Stiles (1999) has further clarified the concept of catalytic validity by framing it in terms of the question: 'Did the research process reorient, focus and energize participants?' In terms of this definition, catalytic validity is *inherent* in a values-based approach given its underlying intentions, provided that deep participation of local stakeholders (e.g. CSO staff) is maintained throughout the process. We would expect discussions about values, which have been conceptualised as modes of conduct or end-states that are personally or socially preferable to their converse, such as the Rokeach (1973) and related tests outlined in the introduction of this book, to be intrinsically more likely to energise participants than discussions about performance indicators or concrete outputs. Furthermore, the very nature of values-based indicators is to *catalyze* focused, collective reflection on whatever it is that individuals and organizations value most. As well as enabling groups to elicit and crystalize their own values, the process often has the effect of turning the spotlight on 'values gaps' (discrepancies between values and practices) and, ultimately, energizing people into changing their behaviour, as described in Chapter 3 in the case of the Juatarhu youth at Echeri. For us, the concept of catalytic validity offers a very important way forward. Our values-based framework is not only offering a means of making intangible social values explicit and measurable, but also challenging underlying assumptions about what counts as valid in evaluation research processes.

In the final part of this book, three detailed case studies are offered, to explore in more depth what kinds of specific processes and outputs can be enabled by a values-based framework, many of which go beyond the original intentions of the ESDinds project. Then, in the conclusion, we will return to the wider questions raised at the beginning of the book, to consider the lessons learnt to date through our work on measuring intangible values. This will involve reflecting on how it also creates potentially transformative learning about values-based approaches and what it means for participatory methods, emergent developmental research frameworks and research through design theories and practice.

References

Cantle, T. (2012) *Interculturalism: For the Era of Cohesion and Diversity*. Basingstoke:Palgrave Macmillan.

Colvert, G. (2007) 'Back to Nature: Aquinas and Ethical Naturalism', *LYCEUM*, VIII(2) Spring.

Crowne, D. P. and Marlowe, D. (1960) 'A New Scale of Social Desirability Independent of Psychopathy', *Journal of Consulting Psychology*, 24, pp. 349–354.

Fisher, R. J. (1993) 'Socially Desirable Responding and the Validity of Indirect Questioning', *Journal of Consumer Research*, 20, pp. 303–315.

Fisher, R. J. and Katz, J. E. (2000) 'Social-Desirability Bias and the Validity of Self-Reported Values', *Psychology & Marketing*, 17, pp. 105–120.

Guba, E. and Lincoln, Y. (1989) *Fourth Generation Evaluation*. Newbury Park, CA: Sage.

Habermas J. (1972) *Knowledge and Human Interests*. London: Heinemann.

Jo, M.-S. (2000) 'Controlling Social-Desirability Bias via Method Factors of Direct and Indirect Questioning in Structural Equation Models', *Psychology & Marketing*, 17, pp. 137–148.

Lather, P. (1986) 'Issues of Validity in Openly Ideological Research: Between a Rock and a Soft Place', *Interchange*, 17, pp. 63–84.

Lincoln, Y. S. and Guba, E., (1985). *Naturalistic Inquiry*. Beverly Hills, CA: Sage.

Messick, S. (1995) 'Validity of Psychological Assessment: Validation of Inferences from Persons' Responses and Performances as Scientific Inquiry into Score Meaning', *American Psychologist*, 50, 741–749.

Onwuegbuzie, A. J., Witcher, A. E., Collins, A. T., Filer, J. D., Wiedmaier, C. D., and Moore, C. W. (2007) 'Students' Perceptions of Characteristics of Effective College Teachers: A Validity Study of a Teaching Evaluation Form Using a Mixed-Methods Analysis', *American Educational Research Journal*, 44, pp. 113–160.

Orne, M. T. (1969). 'Demand Characteristics and the Concept of Quasi-Controls'. In Rosenthal, R. and Rosnow, R. L. (Eds.) *Artifact in Behavioral Research* (pp. 143–179). New York: Academic Press.

"]

Powell, F., and Sze, F. (2004) *Interculturalism: Exploring Critical Issues – The Rise of the West*. Oxford: Inter-disciplinary Press.

Reason, P. and Rowan, J. (1981) 'Issues of Validity in New Paradigm Research'. In Reason, P. and Rowan, J. (Eds.) *Human Inquiry: A Sourcebook of New Paradigm Research*. New York: John Wiley.

Rittel, Horst W. J. and Webber, Melvin M. (1973) 'Dilemmas in a General Theory of Planning', *Policy Sciences*, 4, pp. 155–169.

Rokeach, M. (1973) *The Nature of Human Values*. New York: The Free Press.

Stiles, W. B. (1999) 'Evaluating Qualitative Research', *Evidence Based Mental Health*, 2, pp. 99–101.

Part III

Putting a values-based framework into practice

7   Sustainability and business ethics

The original focus of the ESDinds project was on education for sustainability (ESD) in a global context. This was in the widest possible sense, e.g. including diverse types of CSOs or Non-Governmental Organisations (NGOs) or other fora whose work might directly or indirectly raise or embed awareness of sustainability concepts. However, its focus on intangible shared social values – and thus centrally on ethical principles – constitutes a crucial area of debate and discussion in conversations around transitions to sustainability more widely, that are also important to businesses and other organizations who take these issues seriously.

This is because concerns about the abstract and artificial nature of 'business' values, and their perceived irrelevance to working life, are raised throughout the business management literature. Gruys *et al.* (2008: 833) lament that 'too often the values of organizations show up on laminated cards or wall plaques, rarely heard or seen', while Lencioni's (2002: 113) damning verdict on corporate values statements is that the majority are 'bland, toothless or just plain dishonest', with resulting destructive impacts on employee morale, client satisfaction and managerial credibility. Crucially, deeper and more often shared values transmitted implicitly through other channels such as rituals, drama, stories and symbolic constructions within an organization's culture may contradict those that are explicitly communicated in oral or written forms (Kirkhaug 2009). Even when there is a prominent and unambiguous values discourse within an organization, shared understanding of value meanings may be lacking. Focusing on values can thus backfire, as Cha and Edmondson explain: 'The inherently abstract or "fuzzy" nature of values creates the potential for multiple plausible interpretations of the values' appropriate meanings' (2006: 71). They also describe the problem of 'values expansion': the tendency of employees to add new layers of meaning to the value-labels passed on to them by senior management. This may result in attributions of hypocrisy to leaders even as they continue to remain faithful to their original understandings of the value-labels, and often generates disenchantment – a 'toxic' blend of frustration, anger, disappointment and loss of trust – among employees. Cha and Edmondson speculate that such disenchantment might trigger increased absenteeism, impaired job performance and detrimental effects on work attitudes and behaviours.

Similarly, Lencioni (2002) provides an actual example of a company in which incongruence between leaders' and employees' understandings of a single value-label led directly to the resignation of a senior executive. In this chapter we will explore the central importance of embedding an ethical perspective into businesses, that is transparent, explicit and shared, and demonstrate how a values-based framework can enable organisations to embed sustainability actions in a deep and integrated manner.

Sustainability as an ethical process

Some wishing to make sustainability important in their organisations take the approach of working separately through what has been called the 'three pillars' – environmental, economic and social dimensions – in the hope of eventually creating shifts towards integrated sustainability actions in organisations. However, there have been growing concerns that this three-pillar model of sustainability may be overlooking something of fundamental importance. As highlighted by Littig and Griessler (2005) and more recently by Dahl (2012), there have been several attempts to define this missing dimension as a fourth pillar of sustainability (Burford *et al.* 2013), but it has also been variously described as a cultural–aesthetic, political–institutional or religious–spiritual dimension. Each of these are outlined below.

Cultural–aesthetic

A well-established framing of the fourth pillar, or missing dimension, of sustainability conceptualizes it in terms of culture, the arts and/or aesthetics. Jon Hawkes makes this case explicitly in his book *The Fourth Pillar of Sustainability: Culture's Essential Role in Public Planning* (2001), where he suggests that well-being, creativity, diversity and innovation – what he calls 'cultural vitality', should be treated as one of the basic requirements of a healthy society. While advocating for community involvement in arts practice, Hawkes makes it clear that he is referring to a broader definition of culture that is not limited to arts and heritage, but encompasses the whole complex of distinctive spiritual, material, intellectual and emotional features that characterize a society or social group, as outlined in the UNESCO (1982) *Mexico City Declaration on Cultural Policies*. In addition, many UNESCO publications since the 1990s have highlighted the central role of culture in sustainability – either as a – self-standing pillar of sustainable development or as a foundation underlying the other three pillars. This has been particularly significant within the context of Education for Sustainable Development (ESD), where the cultural pillar has a strong focus on acknowledging and respecting diverse worldviews, identities and local languages and promoting open dialogue and debate.

Political–institutional

The concept of a political-institutional fourth pillar is also widely known. Institutional aspects of sustainability were explicitly addressed in the indicator system developed by the Commission on Sustainable Development (CSD) in 1995 to assess the implementation of Agenda 21 (Pfahl 2005; Spangenberg 2002; Spangenberg *et al.* 2002) as well as being the subject of a dedicated chapter in the Brundtland report *Our Common Future* (WCED 1987). As Spangenberg explains, institutions are the outcome of 'interpersonal processes, such as communication and co-operation, resulting in information and systems of rules governing the interaction of members of a society' (2002: 104). The development of institutional sustainability indicators is rooted in an understanding of institutions that includes, but is not limited to, organizations.

Religious–spiritual

A third, and much lesser known, perspective on the missing pillar/dimension of sustainability is rooted in the concept of an awakening global ethical and spiritual consciousness that underpins sustainability transitions (Clugston 2011; ECI 2010; Hedlund de Witt 2011). In his keynote address at the 2010 Earth Charter conference "An Ethical Framework for a Sustainable World" Steven Rockefeller described this emerging consciousness as 'in truth the *first* pillar of a sustainable way of life', on the grounds that ethical vision and moral courage are essential to generating the political will required for transitions to sustainability (Clugston 2011: 174, emphasis added).

All of these various developments are underpinned by the desire to *start* by nurturing a more holistic ethical and reflective approach; in the hope that this will lead to a natural integration of the 'three pillars' – environment, economics and society – through the concept of values/ethics/culture as a fourth pillar of sustainability. This acknowledgement that values underpin and link sustainability concepts is embedded in our approach, in its use of values-based indicators to conceptualize locally shared values that underpin decisions. The fourth-pillar approach – where the fourth pillar is seen as the interconnecting values/ethics/culture – is less well known precisely because it is difficult to measure. How, then, can we make ethics central, explicit and measurable for businesses and other organisations concerned with sustainability?

Scholars in business ethics have recently identified several similar challenges to those explored in this book in their own areas, such as problems of measurement, rigour and meaningfulness to practitioners; corporate social responsibility; and institutionalization of ethics in businesses. This chapter illustrates how the use of our values-based framework influenced business ethics across eight organizations, apparently and unexpectedly, assisting in the embedding of local ethics. We will argue that multiple specific impacts were found, including (1) deep values conceptualization; (2) increased esteem; (3) building capacity for assessment of values-based achievements; (4) values mainstreaming; and (5) effective external values communications. Although this study was exploratory, it clearly shows that our values-based approach holds promise for meeting key challenges identified in business ethics and wider sustainability challenges, and for new directions for future cross-disciplinary research for moving towards more integrated sustainability actions.

In addition, the work allowed some consideration of broader research through design intentions. When anecdotal accounts of unexpected impacts of the implementation of the values-based approaches began to emerge, the researchers looked more deeply into the relevant related academic and practitioner literature – business ethics – and investigated which design features of the approach were linked to which impacts of interest to others. This sub-research explored dominant paradigms within and across both business and sustainability, and the need to work across 'academic tribes' (Becher and Trowler 1989) and to better integrate conceptual and practical issues. This research through design theme will be returned to in the conclusion to this chapter.

The underlying ethics of sustainability

We have already suggested that the concept of 'ethical values' offers some common ground as a fourth dimension of sustainability that is at least of equal importance to, and actually inseparable from, environmental, economic and societal dimensions. In fact, there have been a number of high-level calls for the establishment of a global ethical framework for sustainability such as by the Earth Charter (Clugston 2011), the United Nations Millennium Declaration (2000) and the Earth Systems Science Partnership (Biermann 2007). More recently, the Club of Rome's 'ValuesQuest' program, linked to the United Nations Culture, Creativity and Values Initiative, has explicitly sought to embed ethical values as a key concern in international development discourse (Palmer and Wagner 2012). Thus, dimensions of values are increasingly being developed in sustainable development.

Organizations and businesses have a central role in the challenge of developing sustainable societies. Already at the turn of the century, Carroll predicted that ethical approaches to business would become a central concern, and emphasized the need for normative approaches to understanding values rather than mere values clarification or 'ethical relativism' (2000: 41). Over a decade later, mission statements, guiding principles, moral standards and Corporate Social Responsibility (CSR) practices and policies, have become commonplace and core to business activities (Holland and Albrecht 2013) and within them, activities related to values have become increasingly popular (von Groddeck 2011).

Nevertheless, problems for the application of ethical values in organizations remain. In 2013, Holland and Albrecht surveyed 3,600 members of business ethics societies and networks to identify key future challenges for the academic field of business ethics research. The results included CSR; perceived challenges with legitimacy and credibility of the field; problems of measurement, rigour and meaningfulness to practitioners; decline of ethical behaviour; and the institutionalization of ethics in businesses. At the same time, however, the project research team started receiving anecdotal evidence suggesting that our values-based evaluative interventions previously undertaken with some business organisations, not only enabled participants to articulate values as individuals and groups, but also led to organizational impacts that far exceeded the expectations of either researchers or collaborators. Considering the potential importance of bringing values effectively into organizational practices, we identified the need for a systematic follow-up study to explore the impacts of the use of our approach, within a broader organizational context – a deviation from the central original focus. However, this study was necessarily exploratory as the original project was not purposively designed to explore such impacts. Rather, it was revealed that analysis of even retrospective information collected post-workshops from organisations yielded important lessons, as well as much material for the future design of a more systematic impact-related investigation (Burford *et al.* 2016).

Purpose, paradigm and context of the study

This follow-up investigation identified impacts seen in eight organizations, from the time of the intervention up until 3–6 months later. This included greatly clarified understanding and awareness of shared values, the mainstreaming of those values into work, and a new ability to self-develop ways of capturing 'measures' of values-related achievements and communicate them more widely. The depth, scale and consistency of the results were noteworthy.

Through increasing our understanding that values awareness is an interpretative process where an individual recognizes moral relevance to their situation (Reynolds 2008) and that moral identity is a precursor to ethical considerations (McFerran *et al.* 2010) we understood that these observed impacts are very relevant to the raising and embedding of ethical considerations into organizations, and to almost every issue identified as a current challenge in business ethics by Holland and Albrecht (2013). Such a focus on values can provide a useful bridge between individuals, organizational culture, practices and behaviours and indeed be seen as an integral part of organizational culture that provides embedded shared guides for tackling complex ethical issues.

This work was based on research approaches that focus on pragmatic questions. The researchers involved examined the impact of the values-based evaluative interventions through detailed case studies, not assuming specific paradigms or theories (again, as before, based on an emergent and grounded theory approach). Here, we focus on the impacts identified related to the values-based framework, beginning with a brief description of the design and content of the approach used in these cases. The methodology of the exploratory impact study is then described, followed by the findings. We conclude by offering a discussion of the findings in relation to three of the named challenges in current business ethics research – institutionalization of ethics, problems with measurements, rigour and relevance and Corporate Social Responsibility (CSR).

Developing and using values-based indicators in organizations

As with many of the other processes outlined in this book, our evaluative work with business organisations was designed as field tests of the developing values-based framework system, that is, as prototyping investigations rather than solutions-driven action research. In particular these evaluations were intended to trial the usefulness and validity of values-based indicators. In this context, the approaches comprised of a number of steps, (with some variations), delivered in the form of meetings, focus groups, workshops or evaluation activities. The format was not fixed, responding to the different contexts and cultures of each organization, but had the following core design elements. After initial familiarization with the organization and building of rapport, researchers initiated conversations about values in the organization, either with leaders or representative groups. Participants were asked to look through a selection of values-based proto-indicators previously developed (as outlined in previous chapters), noting those that resonated with their views on what was important to their own organization. Examples of these proto-indicators, or trigger statements for these particular groups, are shown below: a list derived from in-depth case studies of five organizations (with multiple sub-projects) that was then combined inter-subjectively (Podger *et al.* 2015):

- Decision-making takes into account the social, economic and environmental needs of future generations.
- People are able to suspend their own standpoints during dialogue and listen to those of others.
- People feel that their own individual identity and approach is respected.
- People feel that they have an equal opportunity to express their opinions.
- People are perceived to be transparent.
- People are taking the opportunity to develop their own visions and goals for projects and/or for the whole entity.
- People investigate what is right and good by themselves, rather than adopting other people's opinions.
- Partners trust that each shares a commitment and willingness to collaborate for a similar vision.
- People feel that they create something better or greater as a group than on their own.
- People feel inspired by the way that leaders live their principles.
- The environment/community of life is celebrated.

As with the methodology already outlined in previous chapters, these indicators could then be locally associated (or not) with the value-headings, that had emerged from the very beginning of the project – Empowerment, Justice,

Respect and Care for the Community of Life, Collaboration in Diversity, Justice, Trust/Trustworthiness and Integrity. Any such associations would be considered locally relevant and not transferable to other organizations, but the proto-indicators themselves were found to be useful and transferable as they were designed to be contextualizable for different organizations. For example, the recurring word 'people' could be locally defined as any appropriate stakeholder group, e.g. managers, staff or participants/clients, and could be changed to a more specific term at the users' discretion. The word 'entity' typically meant the organization as a whole, but could also be used to refer to a specific department, team, working group, etc. The group discussions triggered by these proto-indicators led to a convergence of agreed values-in-action with specific localized indicators.

During this stage participants usually found examples relating to previously articulated group thoughts. However, they often also found on the list surprising items which represented values they held but which they were previously not very aware of – causing some 'Eureka!' moments. The group discussions led to clarifications about proto-indicators on the list (values-in-language) and actions in the workplace (values-in-action). After a considerable period of discussion to achieve consensus on final wordings, participants were facilitated to prioritize and sometimes cluster the most important proto-indicators to produce their own 'list of values-based indicators'.

This, then, was the first stage of our approach, which usually had to be separated from the second stage by at least a few days because the participants often experienced significant clarification of their organizational values, and time was needed for acclimatization. The values-in-action which emerged in the workshops were often newly articulated, or even different to those already formally widely espoused. In this second stage, participants were asked which of their own list of values-based proto-indicators they would be interested in developing measures for, depending on their immediate priorities. When identified, the researchers facilitated the participants to co-develop various assessment methods in locally appropriate ways in order to develop 'measures' of those proto-indicators that held relevance and validity for the organization. As with all our work, the approach taken was one of co-design and action research, with a strong focus on face-validity. The participants were supported, in effect, to embed ongoing assessments of their own values in their regular activities at levels of rigour appropriate to the purpose required, for example sometimes for self-evaluation and sometimes for external scrutiny.

Finally, in the third stage, participants and researchers carried out actual assessments, sometimes few and sometimes many, and with varied levels of participation in the collection and analysis of data. All cases included a follow-up interaction with the research team.

How the data was collected and analysed

Through these processes business ethics and sustainability study data was collected from eight organizations using a multiple case study approach (Cohen *et al.* 2011).

This was based on a qualitative thematic analysis of the original dataset, comprising semi-structured narrative interview transcripts and project documents. The cases analysed in this study were selected on the basis of having at least two different data sources available for a particular organization, of which at least one was a semi-structured interview. The data set also included the following from the original ESDinds project field trials: (1) researchers' formal project reports and field notes; (2) transcripts of semi-structured narrative interviews with key informants – organization directors, project managers or both, as practicable – in participating organizations; and (3) transcripts of interviews with the researchers who conducted the field visits and evaluative interventions. All of the post-workshop interviews lasted 60–90 min. and were conducted 3–6 months after the field visits, with a view to eliciting narratives of perceived processes and outcomes during the field visits in participants' own words, without priming for values conceptualization or 'benefits'. This was to avoid compromising validity by imposing preconceptions of what the outcomes might be.

A thematic analysis was then carried out in order to identify predominant themes relating to longer-term potential outcomes of our values-based evaluation framework. After the themes were finalized, the researchers conducted a content analysis for each of the themes, to identify more precisely the occurrence of related impacts and outcomes. Both open and a priori codes were used; the latter were taken from literature on values, semiotics and inter-subjectivity (McFerran *et al.* 2010). The researchers also characterized the findings in terms of their impact relating to managers, staff, or clients involved in the evaluative intervention (Agle and Caldwell 1999).

Values conceptualization

As can be seen in Table 7.1, there was very strong evidence of values conceptualization in all eight organizations studied, (i.e. creating or enhancing experiential understandings of 'values'). This occurred through strengthening of the links between values-in-language (such as named values-labels like Trust, or specific values-based indicators like the examples listed above) and values-in-action. It is also illustrated by the sample quotations given in Table 7.1. Whichever values items were used, by reflecting on them individually and then discussing, exploring, debating and modifying the details of them collectively, participants achieved a deeper and richer shared understanding of how these explicitly articulated and shared values were (or could be) enacted within their organizations. The data revealed that they took this new perspective with them in the following months:

> all participants stated that their consciousness of the presence and importance of values had been greatly heightened, and that after the field visit they tend to look in terms of values at their work and interactions, both individually and organizationally, in a new way.
>
> (ESDinds 2010a)

Table 7.1 Table showing five main impact themes found in interview data from 8 organizations 3–6 months after involvement with the business ethics and sustainability fieldwork, including sub-themes and illustrative quotes

Theme	Sub-themes	Illustrative quotations
Values conceptualization		"all participants stated that their consciousness of the presence and importance of values had been greatly heightened, and that after the field visit they tend to look in terms of values at their work and interactions, both individually and organizationally, in a new way' (Carlos, lead researcher on HV field visit, formal written report).
		'in a region full of sexism, where women do not have that access [to information and decision-making] generally, the youth realized that the project has generated a space of equity. But that [the WeValue approach evaluation] was the moment when they became aware of it…. With the youth, I had been working consciously, very much, around providing that equity, but I never gave them a logo about it: I never said "this is about equity", I just created it' (Maria, DB project manager, face-to-face interview).
		'I think [the youth] got a better understanding of what it is to be involved in [the JGSD global initiative] and that values are the foundations of this movement … It gives them a global picture and a deeper understanding of how you can put into action those values' (Rachel, JGSD project manager; Skype verbal interview).
		Only four JGSD Fundamental Principles were cited by the trainers: humanity (11 times), unity (3 times), independence (1 time) and service (1 time) – compared to respect, which was cited 43 times. This suggests that identifying values is very subjective, but also that the process of identifying values from indicators (more tangible expressions of those values), draws out values that are based on experience rather than ones based on more abstract concepts' (Antonia, lead researcher-consultant on JGSD field visit, formal written report).

continued

Table 7.1 Continued

Theme	Sub-themes	Illustrative quotations
Esteem-related outcomes	Increased understanding and acceptance of self, others, organization, and ecosystem as a whole (all inter-related)	'With respect to the youth, they said it in public, that after this process they understand one another better and they value much more what they're doing. They've always felt very united, but now they know *why* they're united' (Maria, DB director, face-to-face interview). 'Through the processes and assessment tools, we [managers] were able to get a deeper insight into the young people's sense of self, each other and the community. The biggest help for me was an added insight into their motivation, awareness and consciousness of themselves and others, and the connection with the group and the environment' (Maria, as above). 'Professor S. stated that she had observed positive attitudinal changes as a result of the field visit in all participating staff and volunteers and in her own self, in a way she felt was deeply rooted and transformational' (Carlos, lead researcher-consultant on HV field visit, formal written report describing an informal unstructured interview with host CSO manager). 'It was really, really encouraging. [The youth] can see the things that they still have to work on. And then in some places, we could say to them, "There is this gap between you and us [i.e. managers]; what can we do about it?" It felt really good. I was the one who led the conversation. It was positive, I really enjoyed it. They became more self-confident' (Ingrid, QU project manager, face-to-face interview). 'I would say that this has affected them positively in terms of respect for leadership, now they realise that those leaders were not imposing something or showing that they wouldn't improve, but they were the spokesmen or spokeswomen much more' (Rachel, JMSD project officer talking about TMSD field visit, Skype voice call).

Assessment capacity building	Increased understanding and acceptance of indicators and assessment tools (inter-related)	'[At a national youth camp, the youth group members] ran the same process for other youth. They offered it as an ice-breaker activity. They did a spiral of "where are you." [i.e. spatial survey using a spiral] – they chose four indicator questions and asked them, using the spiral' (Maria, DB director, face-to-face interview).
		'They simply liked the assessment tool, and they want to be able to replicate it on their own, so they taped it on a video' (Stefan, assistant researcher-consultant on TMSD field visit, face-to-face interview).
		'what's really good for us is this observation tool. It's simple, easy, objective, this is something we really can use' (Ingrid, QU project manager, face-to-face interview).
Internal transformation/ values mainstreaming	Personal commitment (buy-in)	'It raised awareness of where they should be, what they should be doing in their communities as young people who are actually changing their mindsets, especially with these Principles and Values of JGSD … making a difference within their own communities with their own actions. They seem more mature' (Rachel, JGSD project manager, Skype verbal interview).
	Individual behaviour and group dynamics	'The original indicator was "Group norms exist and they are followed." For that question everybody went into [the part of the spiral that represented the answer] "More or less". We asked them, "Why? You make your own rules, and there is no pressure or imposition of these norms, why don't you respect them?" And as a result of that process the youth made a commitment [to respect them], without me putting any pressure on them, but because they felt ashamed. They promised to follow the norms like arriving on time and keeping the blog updated. It has worked, I am here and they are doing everything! That result transformed the group relationship' (Maria, DB director, face-to-face interview).
	Strategic planning	'As a result of this process we decided that next year we would not do as many activities but we would identify those with the highest impact on selves, communities and ecosystem, thanks to the information provided by the indicators. It helped us to prioritise our activities, we had such a broad spread of action. (Maria, DB director, face-to-face interview).

continued

Table 7.1 Continued

Theme	Sub-themes	Illustrative quotations
	Training	'One of the peer educators said that previously, in presenting the Earth Charter in the workshops she used to focus on concrete behaviours, such as recycling waste. Following the field visit she stated that she now puts a much greater emphasis on the Earth Charter values, and sees the Earth Charter not just as a way of achieving specific behaviours but in terms of the development of the whole individual, beginning with herself, and for participants also' (Carlos, lead researcher-consultant on HV field visit, formal written report describing informal focus group with HV staff).
		'After [the field visit] we changed our preparation phase [for new volunteers] to values. The first week we focused on service, the second week on consultation, the third on being an example, the fourth on consultation, and the fifth on unity.… Before when we did the preparation phase, we just focused on themes, like acting, etc, and each week we would look at a topic connected to QU and the show' (Ingrid, QU project manager, Skype interview).
	Internal communication	'We could see where there were differences between the youth and the staff, especially about information, we could see where the youth especially see that there are difficulties with communication between them and the staff' (Ingrid, QU project manager, Skype interview).
	Individual performance assessment	'I realised that before I was categorising [schools] according to more superficial aspects, and what was missing was the values. That made me realise that we have to impart the value of Respect and Care for the Community of Life right at the start … if that value wasn't there then the commitment or the energy wouldn't be there, even if everything else seemed perfect.… Everything has acquired a clearer lens since the visit' (Maria, DB director, face-to-face interview).
		'[Our previous approach to individual performance assessment] was just my own intuition as a teacher, but without any certitude … I could see values there in the relationships and the commitment, but I couldn't see how it was possible to measure. [In the the WeValue approach process] through dialogue, we were gradually arriving at the complexities and translating it into something marvellously simple that gave deep information' (Maria, DB director, face-to-face interview).

Organizational performance assessment	'The process helped us to understand how we were doing in relation to assimilation of the values that we promoted as a core goal, both for the entire project and in each of the participating schools' (Maria, DB director, face-to-face interview).
External dissemination — Donors	'Thanks to this process, [our major donor] has reconceptualized the work of DB as something of *international* relevance, no longer just a local project' (Maria, DB director, face-to-face interview). '[DB's major donor] was very interested. They asked me if I would be interested in developing an entire indicator system for their national work, tailor-made, as opposed to the generic the WeValue approach one' (Carlos, lead researcher-consultant on DB field visit, face-to-face interview).
Existing partners/clients	'In the schools it worked, the process was very helpful, in particular helping the teachers and the headmasters to understand that my work is not just teaching the children how to plant trees, but also in values. It helped in the relationships with the institutions. The schools saw that we were creating respect for the community of life' (Maria, DB director, face-to-face interview).
Prospective partners/clients	'It would make it easier for new schools who think about working with us. It's sometimes hard for us to explain what goes on in our performances. We normally have to give them a live example, show them a full performance so that they can see an example of what we do, and then they decide. It works, but it's very time-consuming. If we can measure values, we can give them more clarity' (Josef, QU director, face-to-face interview).
Policy-makers	'We nearly had a couple of meetings with the President. We did have a meeting with the Minister for Education and Youth who had a behaviour change programme which the President is very close to. They were very interested in the WeValue approach. That was also part of what helped the process of assimilation. Because at that meeting it wasn't just us presenting it, but also [local managers], particularly A. presenting the WeValue approach as he understood it to the government, in terms of the relevance that he felt' (Carlos, lead researcher-consultant on TMSD field visit, face-to-face interview). 'since we met our national secretariat here and we spoke about these values indicators and the measurement of these values indicators, and [in] their own jargon now, every time they come on to the media that's all that they're talking about' (Ibrahim, TMSD project manager, Skype text interview).

Source: adapted from Burford *et al.* (2016) 'An Unexpected Means of Embedding Ethics in Organizations: Preliminary Findings from Values-based Evaluations', *Sustainability*, 8, p. 612.

In some cases the values-based indicators which were discussed and refined were similar to the values espoused in pre-existing documents such as mission statements and websites, but in other cases they were very different interpretations or even entirely new 'core values' that had not previously been acknowledged or discussed. Several examples were seen of underlying values which were key to group work – but previously unarticulated – being elicited and then verbalized:

> in a region full of sexism, where women do not have that access (to information and decision-making) generally, the youth realized that the project has generated a space of equity. But that (the evaluative intervention) was the moment when they became aware of it.... With the youth, I had been working consciously, very much, around providing that equity, but I never gave them a logo about it: I never said 'this is about equity', I just created it.
>
> (ESDinds 2010b)

Beyond the distinct processes discussed above, namely the addition of referents to specific value-labels and vice-versa, we also found evidence for a broader, slower and 'fuzzier' values conceptualization and awareness-raising effect arising from the original intervention. This seemed to begin with an enhanced general awareness that values did indeed underlie day-to-day actions within the organization, moving to a realization that they could be made visible through values-based evaluation, and thus to a reinforcement that values provided a useful and relevant framework with which to view their work. It was reported from one group, for example:

> I think (the youth) got a better understanding of what it is to be involved in (the JGSD global initiative) and that values are the foundations of this movement.... It gives them a global picture and a deeper understanding of how you can put into action those values.
>
> (ESDinds 2010b)

Although assessment capacity is mentioned below as a separate impact category, it is worth noting the finding that when the organizations performed assessments of their values-based indicators and then had before them 'measures' indicating the extent of their presence, that this had a visible reinforcement effect in some cases. The quote about 'equity' above is an example: assessment results reinforced that it was present and reminded participants of its importance to them.

Esteem-related outcomes

The original interventions also contributed to deepening people's understanding, acceptance and valuing of themselves, one another, and the group or organization. These ranged from improvements in the self-esteem of individual managers or employees, through changes in the way in which managers understood and valued their staff (or vice-versa), to new understandings of the significance of the organization's work. The distinction between general values conceptualization and these esteem-related outcomes may not always be entirely clear. However, we see the former more as the development of a values-based lens with many components, whereas the latter are consequences, e.g. new ways of viewing colleagues and work through that new lens:

> This project helped us a lot and it still helps. We try to think about what is the value behind (participants' actions).... This is how we see each human being, full of values.
>
> (Ibid.)

Some interviewees also commented explicitly, and others implied, that these outcomes have a strong morale-boosting effect. Thus, reflection on one positive outcome could generate others. In one case an organization was inspired by Indigenous environmental values and the director suggested that the intervention had changed not only the participants' view of their own organization but also their understanding and awareness of the human-environment system within their forest.

Our qualitative data contain several examples of improved relationships between managers and staff, improved self-esteem and specifically 'feeling understood and valued' (ibid.).

Assessment capacity building

In the second stage of the original interventions, participants were facilitated to understand and develop assessment tools to produce measures of the indicators they had prioritized. In many cases, assessment tools were designed to fit in closely with the day-to-day activities of the organizations. The degree of rigour and type of validity required was discussed and varied depending on the specific needs of each group. Some indicators had only single, informal measures for one aspect, while others had several assessments, designed to provide a more rigorous evaluation. At this point we had not considered that the organizations might make a sustained use of the assessment methods developed, beyond the length of our project, or be able to go further and develop new ones in the future.

Our findings showed however that, several months later, a number of organizations had continued to use – and, in a few cases, even extended – the assessment methods they had used during their work with us. Thus, there was an unexpected impact of our values-based framework in building capacity in performance assessment. Managers and their staff showed that they could learn new ways of understanding and evaluating the intangible shared values of individuals and of the whole organization: in ways which resonate with them and instil a feeling of ownership. Some of the organizations' managers, staff and even clients acquired new understandings of the concept and uses of indicators, and of specific assessment methods. In two case study organisations, managers and clients were empowered to use our evaluative approach independently in different contexts. As these were non-profit groups that were not previously comfortable with performance assessment (beyond their formal donor-driven evaluation requirements) this was a significant and unexpected outcome. The experience of the original intervention inspired organizations accustomed to quantitative evaluation to explore qualitative and creative ways of understanding impact. Conversely, small organizations who have avoided formal evaluation found our approach an attractive alternative which encouraged them to adopt systematic surveys and observations.

Values mainstreaming and internal transformation

Considering the findings discussed above of values conceptualization and awareness raising, increased value of self and others, and increased ability to determine measures of values in everyday activities, it is perhaps not surprising that the researchers also found evidence of the joint impact of these into a higher-level impact of values mainstreaming, i.e. the shifting of the organization to a more 'values-based management' approach. Evidence was found of observable changes in the following arenas: assessment of individual and/or organizational performance; strategic planning; internal communications; and training protocols. Internal transformation, while encompassing all of the above, is a broader category that can also include changes in 'buy-in' or commitment to the organization and its activities, as well as changes in individual behaviour and group dynamics – not necessarily directly values-based. Increased buy-in, changes to strategic planning processes, improvements in individual behaviour and group dynamics, and changes to training, assessment and internal communications protocols were all observed at the managerial level in more than one case study. At the staff level, increased buy-in was observed in several cases, and each of the other named outcomes was evident in one of the case studies.

Among participants/clients (e.g. beneficiary youth groups), both 'increased buy-in' and 'changes in individual behaviour and group dynamics' were also observed in more than one case study. As already outlined in Chapter 4, It is possible that by illuminating 'value-action gaps', our approach may serve as a catalyst for self-directed individual behaviour change without the need for authoritarian managerial intervention, a theme that needs exploring further in future work. Of particular interest is the example of concrete behaviour change cited in one organization, where the members of the youth group recognized through the participatory evaluation that they were failing to meet their own self-imposed norms. As a result, and without any direct intervention from their manager, they changed their behaviour in order to conform more fully to the standards that they had set themselves. This, in turn, transformed the group dynamics.

External communications

As might be expected from transformational work on organizational values, important subsequent external communication activities took place between organization managers and their counterparts in partner organizations, such as the head teachers of schools participating in an environmental project. There were also significant and intriguing single-case examples of new styles of communication to donors and policy-makers in two of the organizations. The interview data hint at secondary outcomes occurring within these recipient organizations and institutions, which in turn have gone on to adopt value-labels and other related referents into their own vocabularies. The major donor to one of the groups has since commissioned a large multi-level evaluation of its own national programs using our approach. The data shows that new understandings generated can catalyze change within the organization in question, and also transform the way in which the organization presents itself to others.

Our approach and its impact on business ethics

The findings detailed above clearly illustrate how our original interventions helped organizations contribute to a number of key issues identified in business ethics research. Some of the challenges mentioned by Holland and Albrecht (2013) are directly addressed, such as problems of measurement, rigour, and meaningfulness to practitioners; the institutionalization of ethics in businesses; and CSR. We first discuss the linkages to these named challenges, and then consider linkages to some conversations in the wider business ethics literature.

Problems of measurement, rigour and meaningfulness to practitioners

Fundamental to the usefulness of our approach is its ability to efficiently facilitate participants to articulate explicitly in discourse what they already undertake or experience together as values-in-practice. In that way, they jointly develop values-based indicators – short sentences that clarify a manifestation of a shared value. This process helps to concretize values that underpin decisions about what is or is not ethical. Once produced, the same indicators effectively provided criteria for the practice and application of ethics – which can also be used to devise informal or formal 'measures' that are valid to the participants and adapted to the context. Organizations that had previously eschewed evaluation methods of any kind enthusiastically developed localized assessment methods to provide 'measures' of these indicators which then informed observable practices of individuals and groups – precisely because they considered the indicators very meaningful to them and the measures a mechanism for self-evaluation and learning. The levels of rigor used depended on the purpose: in some cases three assessment methods were used for one sole indicator, which itself might be only one of a set of 10–12 indicators designated – locally, by that organization – to be elements of one core value. The measures developed for those 12 indicators could then provide a meaningful and rigorous representation of that core value to members of the organization, their stakeholders or funders. In other cases, participants used a simple measure of fewer indicators, giving more importance to the localized statement itself rather than an overarching label. Regardless, the purposefully designed localizability of indicators, and flexibility in choice and design of assessment methods, provided local solutions to the challenges of defining ethical and sustainable values for the practitioners involved in these eight organizations. This process does not exclude external evaluations: external evaluators could be allowed to specify other indicators from the locally derived pool, or still use their own.

Institutionalization of ethics

The institutionalization of ethics in organizations as described by experts in the field of business ethics broadly refers to developing strong ethical cultures and a clear focus on how to apply ethics in all practices of the organization. The findings from this exploratory study suggest that clearly conceptualizing shared organizational values – through meaningful discussion – and developing concrete indicators to effectively define them in practice, led to mainstreaming of values in the organization. The fact that the indicators were designed to be operationalizable, and that the participants co-developed specific assessment tools for the values-based indicators may be key: they might have effectively integrated different ways of understanding ethical values in everyday practices. The contextually developed values-based indicators became reference items, not only for possible evaluation, but also for guiding ethical judgments during decision-making processes. Furthermore, the participatory nature of our approach, which included deep discussions leading to the conceptualization of shared values, and involvement in the evaluative process, gave space for reflection on developments in the organizations' ethical culture.

Corporate social responsibility

The values conceptualization, mainstreaming and external communication impacts of our approach have important implications for the understanding and application of CSR in organizations. The indicators approach allowed for the conceptualization and operationalization of the organization's values, in turn providing clear guidance for managers, staff and beneficiaries on the actual practices that support CSR within the organization and helping to move 'from rhetoric on business ethics and CSR to meaningful action' (Holland and Albrecht 2013: 783). In addition, the values-based indicators and their measures provide potential for generating measures of ethics and CSR practices, and can provide innovative and meaningful ways of communicating such practices.

Values conceptualization and mainstreaming can generate diverse examples of a company's commitment to values –and provide conceptual and strategic frameworks for reporting CSR. This is a valuable tool for companies faced with an increasingly cynical public wanting evidence of the triple bottom line (Christofi *et al.* 2012) and critical of empty values statements not backed up by action (Du *et al.* 2010). Indeed, while 64 per cent of the 250 largest multinational companies published Corporate Social Responsibility (CSR) reports in 2005, review shows that the majority of them listed multiple uncoordinated initiatives rather than elucidating a coherent strategy (Foote *et al.* 2010). In this context, our approach thus appears capable of providing a values-based strategy, and clear indicators for internal and external communication, monitoring and evaluation.

Values in organizations: towards ethics in practice

Although a relatively new focus in sustainability research, the concept of values has long been central for business ethics, management and organization studies. In an effort to study the challenge of applying ethics in practice, a number of researchers have focused on behavioural ethics approaches, investigating the influence of values held by individuals within an organization, with evidence that these can influence employee behaviour and decision-making processes. Values have been described as a key element of exemplary leadership (Kemaghan 2003), a way for managers to influence individual behaviour without resorting to authoritarianism (Buchko 2007), and an important mediator in decisions about equal resource allocation (Garcia *et al.* 2010). Enhanced values focus in management has also been shown to increase trust and understanding between managers and their subordinates (Artto *et al.* 2011; Christensen *et al.* 2012).

This is in contrast to approaches in organization studies, which focus on values at the organizational level. Such research provides evidence for the influence of collective values – and how these are perceived – on those working within organizations. In their study of 902 managers from different contexts, Huhtala *et al.* (2011) demonstrate that there is a positive relationship between managers' perceptions of ethical organizational culture and occupational well-being. Other studies have demonstrated the positive effects of congruence between individual and organizational values on staff retention, satisfaction and increased ethical behaviour (Andrews *et al.* 2011; Verquer *et al.* 2003). Indeed, values can be seen as an integral part of organizational culture that provide everday, shared guides for tackling complex ethical issues (von Groddeck 2011).

This study also provided some insights to this research, and links between their different aspects. For example, the impact findings show how collective conceptualization and later evaluation of values-based achievements has effectively united individuals, defining and reinforcing shared values, and collectively clarifying which activities are within or not within their boundaries. That effect could be seen as the focusing of the workforce on clarified mission statements; managers and staff alike. The importance of the elicitation of unarticulated values-in-action into tangible values statements demonstrated in our approach also suggests that a distinction might need to be made in research generally between those and the more superficial values words used in everyday language without prior reflection. This could help clarify some of issues raised by business ethics literature, as outlined in the introduction to this chapter. In fact, findings from other studies might be negated in cases where individuals do not have shared values-in-action to build on but are trying to reconcile superficial values with no grounding in a context-specific reality. In such cases, values-based approaches might not only be non-useful but could easily lead to misunderstandings and even polarization of differences. The success of our approach at triggering conceptualization and the production of indicators that are deemed valid by participants thus suggests engagement with values concepts deserves further study across business ethics research. Engaging with a framework such as ours enables a way of moving beyond values being poorly conceptualized; left below the level of full conscious awareness (Agle and Caldwell 1999); being based on individuals' own tacit or explicit understandings of meaning (since collectively agreed definitions are lacking); or ignoring how values understandings vary according to ethnicity, previous life experiences and current circumstances, as well as being highly context-dependent (Brown and Crace 1996; Peng *et al.* 1997).

Another important insight for the wider business community around ethics from our approach is contextualization. As already described in other chapters, early on in our development, it became clear that we needed to steer away from a rigid toolkit and process to a more generative framework or system which could be localized and thus 'owned' rather than seen as an external imposition. This successful localization of values-based indicators is only possible with the contribution provided by members of the organizations when they collectively reflect on their own actions – concretely contextualized in the workplace.

Business ethics concerns itself with the application of certain values that are related to deliberate decisions about what is or is not ethical in a given context. Thus, ethics and related organizational values are arguably more explicit and purposefully linked to practices and behaviours. In practice, this has been translated by the development of codes of ethics as mechanisms for ensuring such practices. However, codes and compliance-based approaches have also been criticized and, akin to values discourses, remain vague and lack specificity (Warren *et al.* 2014). Furthermore, what is ethical in a given organization is defined contextually and will not depend solely on a code (Christensen and Lægreid 2011). In this context, there has been increasing interest in understanding *ethics as practice*, in other words that organizational ethics are constructed through a multiplicity or behaviours, decisions, interpersonal interactions that 'not only embed and enact ethics but also form the framework for their institutionalization, politicization and contestation' (Clegg *et al.* 2007: 94). This way of understanding ethics may contribute to challenges faced by scholars looking at organizational values. Language-based approaches alone do not necessarily generate tangible long-term outcomes (Warren *et al.* 2014). The focus merely on the level of values discourse is limiting: related practices can also influence ethical organizational culture and specific behaviours such as willingness to report unethical behaviours.

The relatively limited evidence provided in this exploratory study of business ethics suggests, provisionally, that our approach may contribute to the development of ethical cultures in organizations. Existing literature also hints at possible ways to do this: Gruys *et al.* (2008) suggest, for example, that a potential solution might be to obtain a measure of organizational values enactment by linking statements of espoused values directly to formal performance assessment systems. That measurement-based approach contrasts with Cha and Edmondson's more constructionist recommendation (2006: 75) of 'thoughtful dialogue' between managers and employees about the meanings and practical implications of value-labels. In a more recent paper, Warren *et al.* (2014) argue that ethics training that examines practices related to ethical dilemmas in detail have more lasting effects than merely focusing on vague codes of ethics and organizational values. All of these studies are consistent with the impact findings reported here, which seem to go further and produce an embryonic framework to understand them. The successful application of ethical values in organizations is of crucial importance for contributions of business and civil society to sustainable development. Business ethics scholars and practitioners have been at the forefront of such work in the past decades. In this chapter we have aimed to show how our approach produced impacts that contribute significantly to current challenges in business ethics, starting with increased awareness and the institutionalization of values in the organizations, with related domino effects on ethics in discourse, communication and action.

Making paradigms in business ethics research explicit

We'd like to end this chapter with some comments on the challenges of trying to work across academic domains and silos, quite apart from the practitioner–academic divide that our work engages with head-on. A very useful overview of paradigms present in and across business ethics and organization theory has been published by Heugens and Scherer (2010) charting not only their boundaries and divisions but also the artificial curtailment of those boundaries, caused by the historical development of various semi-estranged research communities. Although the main intention of that work was to draw out the symbiosis between business ethics and organization theory, a secondary aim was achieved in showing that the pluralism of paradigms and approaches currently present produces a double-edged sword: flexibility and resilience via the range of tools available on the one hand, and a lack of coherence or orientation due to ongoing incompatibilities and even incommensurability on the other hand. This suggested four major themes in the discipline – values, society, power and organizations – from each of modern, symbolic and post-modern viewpoints. Two themes which are of particular interest to us in our own work – values and organizations – were shown to be viewable as individualist or collectivist, almost entirely positivist or constructionist, or anywhere in between, depending on the scholarly community of the researcher. As is Chapter 5, we end with a call to arms for researchers to make greater efforts to engage in science as a social practice and jointly work together across academic 'tribes', thus accessing rich sources of new knowledge. The complex paradigmatic status of the field of business ethics illustrates the difficulties that researchers from other disciplines, such as our consortium, may encounter when trying to communicate concepts and findings which may be of potential interest. This is further complicated by the fact that sustainability research itself is characterized by a diversity of paradigms and perspectives (Robinson 2004; Waas *et al.* 2011; Pryshlakivsky and Searcy 2012). The way that we have taken in this chapter of negotiating this inherently messy interface, is to focus initially on pragmatic considerations before expanding into the various theoretical domains and their associated literature, with the aim of illuminating critical issues, as well as framing directions for future work. Like Holland and Albrecht (2013) we also emphasize the need for an appropriate blend of academic rigor and practical relevance, leaning towards a call for a pragmatist paradigm, where sustainability, the decline of ethical behaviour and globalization are all candidate issues replete with practical questions of ethics in need of answers. We hope that the study outlined here indicates one way forward to take on these crucial concerns.

References

Agle, B. R. and Caldwell, C. B. (1999) 'Understanding Research on Values in Business: A Level of Analysis Framework', *Business & Society*, 38, pp. 326–387.
Andrews, C. M., Baker, T., and Hunt, T. G. (2011) 'Values and Person-Organization Fit: Does Moral Intensity Strengthen Outcomes?' *Leadership & Organization Development Journal*, 32, pp. 5–19.
Artto, K., Kulvika, I., Poskelab, J., and Turkulainen, V. (2011) 'The Integrative Role of the Project Management Office in the Front End of Innovation', *International Journal of Project Management*, 29, pp. 408–421.
Becher, T., and Trowler, P. R. (1989) *Academic Tribes and Territories*. Buckingham and Philadephia: SRHE and Open University Press.
Biermann, F. (2007) '"Earth system governance" as a crosscutting theme of global change research', *Global Environmental Change*, 17, pp. 326–337.
Brown, D. and Crace, R. K. (1996) 'Values in Life Role Choices and Outcomes: A Conceptual Model', *Career Development Quarterly*, 44, pp. 211–223.
Buchko, A. A. (2007) The Effect of Leadership on Values-Based Management. *Leadersh. Organizational Developement Journal*, 20, pp. 36–50.
Burford, G., Hoover, E., Stapleton, L., and Harder, M. (2016) 'An Unexpected Means of Embedding Ethics in Organizations: Preliminary Findings from Values-Based Evaluations', *Sustainability*, 8(7), 612.
Burford, G., Hoover, E., Velasco, I., Janoušková, S., Jimenez, A., Piggot, G., Podger, D., and Harder, M. K. (2013) 'Bringing the "Missing Pillar" into Sustainable Development Goals: Towards Intersubjective Values-Based Indicators', *Sustainability*, 5.
Carroll, A. B. (2000) 'Ethical Challenges for Business in the New Millennium: Corporate Social Responsibility and Models of Management Morality', *Business Ethics Quarterly*, 10, pp. 33–42.
Cha, E. S. and Edmondson, A. C. (2006) 'When Values Backfire: Leadership, Attribution, And Disenchantment in a Values-Driven Organization', *Leadership Quarterly*, 17, pp. 57–78.

Christensen, T. and Lægreid, P. (2011) 'Ethics and Administrative Reforms', *Public Management Review*, 13, pp. 459–477.

Christofi, A., Christofi, P., and Sisaye, S. (2012) 'Corporate Sustainability: Historical Development and Reporting Practices', *Management Research*, 35, pp. 157–172.

Clegg, S., Kornberger, M., and Rhodes, C. (2007) 'Business Ethics as Practice', *British Journal of Management*, 18, pp. 107–122.

Clugston, R. (2011) 'Ethical Framework for a Sustainable World: Earth Charter Plus 10 Conference and Follow Up', *Journal of Education for Sustainable Development*, 5, pp. 173–176.

Cohen, L., Manion, L., and Morrison, K. (2011) *Research Methods in Education*, 7th edn. London: Routledge.

Dahl, A. L. (2012) 'Achievements and Gaps in Indicators for Sustainability', *Ecological Indicators*, 17, pp. 14–19.

Du, S., Bhattacharya, C. B., and Sen, S. (2010) 'Maximising Business Returns to Corporate Social Responsibility (CSR): The Role of CSR Communication', *International Journal of Management Review*, 12, pp. 8–19.

ECI Secretariat. (2010) *Earth Charter Initiative Handbook*. San José, Costa Rica: Earth Charter International Secretariat.

ESDinds (2010a) ESDinds Working Paper: *Report of Field Visit to Organisation 'Hv' for Testing of Set 1 Sustainable Development Indicators*. Brighton, UK: University of Brighton.

ESDinds (2010b) Face-to-face interview with 'Maria' (pseudonym), project manager for organisation 'DB', Skype verbal interview with 'Rachel' (pseudonym), project officer of organisation 'JGSD', and Skype verbal interview with 'Ingrid', project manager of organisation 'QU', in ESDinds Working Paper: *Transcripts of Anonymised Semi-Structured Interviews with Participants in Field Tests of Set 1 Sustainable Development Indicators* (companion material to ESDinds Deliverable 11), G. Burford (Ed.). Brighton, UK: University of Brighton.

Foote, J., Gaffney, N., and Evans, J. R. (2010) 'Corporate Social Responsibility: Implications for Performance Excellence', *Total Quality Management & Business Excellence*, 21, pp. 799–812.

Garcia, S. M., Bazerman, M. H., Kopelman, S., Tor, A., and Milleret, D. T. (2010) 'The Price of Equality: Suboptimal Resource Allocations Across Social Categories'. *Business Ethics Quarterly*, 20, pp. 75–88.

Gruys, M. L., Stewart, S. M., Goodstein, J., and Wick, A. (2008) 'Values Enactment in Organizations: A Multi-Level Examination', *Journal of Management*, 34, pp. 806–843.

Hawkes, J. (2001) *The Fourth Pillar of Sustainability: Culture's Essential Role in Public Planning*. Victoria, Australia: Common Ground Publishing Pty Ltd in association with the Cultural Development Network.

Hedlund-de Witt, A. (2011) 'The Rising Culture and Worldview of Contemporary Spirituality: A Sociological Study of Potentials and Pitfalls for Sustainable Development', *Ecological Economics*, 70, pp. 1057–1065.

Heugens, P. P. M. A. R. and Scherer, A. G. (2010) 'When Organization Theory Met Business Ethics: Toward Further Symbioses', *Business Ethics Quarterly*, 20, pp. 643–672.

Holland, D. and Albrecht, C. (2013) 'The Worldwide Academic Field of Business Ethics: Scholars' Perceptions of the Most Important Issues', *Journal of Business Ethics*, 117, pp. 777–788.

Huhtala, M., Feldt, T., Lämsä, A.-M., Mauno, S., and Kinnunen, U. (2011) 'Does the Ethical Culture of Organisations Promote Managers' Occupational Well-Being? Investigating Indirect Links via Ethical Strain', *Journal Of Business Ethics*, 101, pp. 231–247.

Kemaghan, K. (2003) 'Integrating Values into Public Service: The Values Statement as Centerpiece', *Public Administration Review*, 63, pp. 711–719.

Kirkhaug, R. (2009) 'The Management of Meaning – Conditions for Perception of Values in a Hierarchical Organization', *Journal Of Business Ethics*, 87, pp. 317–324.

Lencioni, P. M. (2002) 'Make Your Values Mean Something', *Harvard Business Review*, 80, pp. 113–117.

Littig, B. and Griessler, E. (2005) 'Social Sustainability: A Catchword Between Political Pragmatism and Social Theory', *International Journal of Sustainable Development*, 8, pp. 65–79.

McFerran, B., Acquino, K., and Duffy, M. (2010) 'How Personality and Moral Identity Relate to Individuals' Ethical Ideology', *Business Ethics Quarterly*, 20, pp. 35–56.

Palmer, M. and Wagner, K. (2012) *ValuesQuest: The Search for Values Which Will Make a World of Difference*. Zurich, Switzerland: The Club of Rome.

Peng, K. P., Nisbett, R. E., and Wong, N. Y. C. (1997) 'Validity Problems Comparing Values Across Cultures and Possible Solutions', *Psychological Methods*, 2, pp. 329–344.

Pfahl, S. (2005) 'Institutional Sustainability', *International Journal of Sustainable Development*, 8, pp. 80–96.

Podger, D., Hoover, E., Burford, G., Hak, T., and Harder, M. K. (2015) 'Revealing Values in a Complex Environmental Program: A Scaling Up of Values-Based Indicators', *Journal of Cleaner Products*.

Pryshlakivsky, J. and Searcy, C. (2012) Sustainable Development as a Wicked Problem. In Kovacic, S. F. and Sousa-Poza, A., (Eds.) *Managing and Engineering in Complex Situations* (pp. 109–128). Dordrecht, the Netherlands: Springer.

Reynolds, S. J. (2008) 'Moral Attentiveness: Who Pays Attention to the Moral Aspects Of Life?' *Journal of Applied Psychology*, 93, pp. 1027–1041.

Robinson, J. (2004) 'Squaring the Circle? Some Thoughts on the Idea of Sustainable Development', *Ecological Economics*, 48, pp. 369–384.

Spangenberg, J. H. (2002) 'Institutional Sustainability Indicators: An Analysis of the Institutions in Agenda 21 and a Draft Set of Indicators for Monitoring Their Effectivity', *Sustainable Development*, 10, pp. 103–115.

Spangenberg, J. H., Pfahl, S., and Deller, K. (2002) 'Towards Indicators for Institutional Sustainability: Lessons from an Analysis Of Agenda 21', *Ecological Indications*, 2, pp. 61–77.

UNESCO (n.d.) *Culture in the Post-2015 Sustainable Development Agenda: Why Culture Is Key to Sustainable Development*. Retrieved from www.unesco.org/new/en/culture/themes/culture-and-development/hangzhou-congress/, Accessed 21 April 2018.

UNESCO (1982) *Mexico City Declaration on Cultural Policies*. Retrieved from www.ifa.de/fileadmin/pdf/abk/inter/unesco_mondiacult.pdf. Accessed 21 April 2018.

United Nations General Assembly (2000) *United Nations Millennium Declaration*. New York: United Nations General Assembly.

Verquer, L. M., Beehr, T. A., and Wagner, S. H. (2003) 'A Meta-Analysis of Relations Between Person-Organization Fit and Work Attitudes', *Journal of Vocational Behaviour*, 63, pp. 473–489.

Von Groddeck, V. (2011) 'Rethinking the Role of Value Communication in Business Corporations from a Sociological Perspective – Why Organisations Need Value-Based Semantics to Cope with Societal and Organisational Fuzziness', *Journal of Business Ethics*, 100, pp. 69–84.

Waas, T., Hugé, J., Verbruggen, A., and Wright, T. (2011) 'Sustainable Development: A Bird's Eye View', *Sustainability*, 3, pp. 1637–1661.

Warren, E. D., Gaspar, J. P., and Laufer, W. F. (2014) 'Is Formal Ethics Training Merely Cosmetic? A Study of Ethics Training and Ethical Organizational Culture', *Business Ethics Quarterly*, 24, pp. 85–117.

World Commission on Environment and Development (1987) Towards Common Action: Proposals for Institutional and Legal Change. In *Our Common Future: Report of the World Commission on Environment and Development*. Geneva, Switzerland: United Nations.

8   Mapping social legacies

A core requirement for many organizations is to map effects and impacts beyond the life of a particular project or initiative. This is likely to be a formal demand from funders, but is also vital to developing values-in-action that are sustainable, robust and really do have an effect on events. This chapter describes a case study of using our values-based approach not only to map the legacies that project groups had initially aspired to, but also, through cross-group collaboration, to make explicit previously vague and intangible legacy aims and measures and to generate additional legacy impact statements. It involved collaborative research projects funded through the Arts and Humanities Research Council (AHRC) Connected Communities programme (Facer and Enright 2016). The AHRC is the main funder of academic research in Arts & Humanities in the UK, but the Connected Communities programme was a funding scheme that looked to support and investigate types of community–university partnerships that went beyond the conventional researcher–civil society organization (CSO) or researcher–client relationships that underpinned their other funding streams. Rather, these projects aimed to involve community partners as holders of legitimate knowledge about, and significant contributors to, research not centred in academia but in wider life. As part of this innovation, the AHRC wanted to understand how its programme could also help support and legitimise ways of knowing that are often marginalised by conventional evaluations, through eliciting and then communicating a comprehensive range of impacts across all project partners and participants.

A key finding from our study in this context has been to recognize an explicit conceptualization of legacy in terms of values. The *Oxford English Dictionary* defines a legacy as 'something left or handed down by a predecessor'. This definition clearly implies a values judgment, in deciding what is 'left' or 'handed down'. The outcomes of a typically funded project are normally defined by the values that motivated its design (that is, the values that the project started with), and for academic funders these centre on academic outputs such as contributions to formal systems of knowledge, typically contained in published papers, books or performances. However, unlike these kinds of outcomes, the notion of *legacy* is based on subjective values of the people involved. Legacies of a project are typically viewed using the same values-lens as the project and its outcomes, but in fact they can be identified and viewed through a variety of different lenses. In our study, appropriately named *Starting from Values: Evaluating Intangible Legacies* (Hoover and Harder 2016), we demonstrated that it is possible to reveal a broader spectrum of legacies by explicitly identifying the different lenses of different actors, who hold different values. Ultimately we suggest that the term 'legacy' may be more important than 'impact' in capturing and communicating the wider and more intangible values and effects of such projects.

As with our previous uses of our values-based approach, the aim was to make values explicit. Since these projects involved partnerships of academics and several different CSOs via representatives, each partnership contained different values sets. The AHRC programme framework (through its selection processes) had assembled groups whose values overlapped in part with others in the partnership, but also varied. Our *Starting from Values* (SfV)[1] framework allowed participants to identify different legacies depending on their values starting point, and provided a systematic way of investigating this. In the further development of this action research, the values approach unravelled even more information. We found that articulating legacies in this way demands that we take a step back and think across outcomes and impacts, by making explicit values judgments about what is important beyond the life of the project, or what the team, or partners want it to 'hand down'. In this way, many previously unidentified outcomes and impacts were found linked to the newly recognized legacies. Because our approach allows different actors to articulate their values and thus legacies seen by them, academic legacies can stand humbly beside those of the CSOs, community groups, local government and wider public. This 're-sets' the balance between academic and the community, and provides a mechanism for understanding and valuing different perspectives. It also gives space and a language to articulate less 'tangible' aspects of project legacies. This means that a values-based approach to understanding the legacies of community-engaged research can:

- reveal legacies as seen by different actors;
- unearth 'new' legacies and a deeper understanding of 'known' legacies;
- enhance existing legacies;
- create confidence to articulate broader and deeper aspects of legacies;
- enhance collaborative working within partnerships;
- put academic legacies into the context of wider societal legacies.

The study also led to additional benefits for the community partners, just as we had found with previous work: energising key members of staff and helping to articulate the values of their own organisations. This has also led to them being better equipped to negotiate their role in future partnership work, inspired participants to develop new projects with values approaches at the heart of design and delivery, and led to new research ideas and practices.

Revealing groups' intangible legacies

Our *Starting from Values* project was structured around two strands:

1 In-depth work on the legacies of two separate Connected Communities community–university partnership projects – 'Scaling Up Co-Design' and the 'Authority Research Network' (ARN) including co-investigating work with each of their partnership members;
2 Learning from this strand, as well as other activities, so as to develop our framework and to work with a further six Connected Communities projects.

These two strands were not consecutive, as we took advantage of existing work and opportunities in the short lifecycle of the AHRC funded programme. For instance, the team developed activities for a Connected Communities Festival (Cardiff 2014), where all the groups came together for an AHRC-organised event, very early on in our work. The study was also structured around a series of five iterative reflections, to bring together learning from it's different strands and develop joint overarching thinking on values approaches around legacies. The last iteration involved a public event to share findings of the project team to date and get additional insights from participants from other backgrounds. An important aspect of the SfV project was for our own community-university partners to co-develop expertise in 'starting from values' in their own projects, and then to also lead activities with other partnership projects and organisations. This second ripple, 'meta-design' aspect of the project helped to build capacity in values-based approaches and evaluation.

In strand one we worked with 'Scaling Up Co-design' which focused on co-design practices within civil society organisations working in different fields (built environment, media and technology), seeking to understand how these practices and their impact on people and society can be scaled up. It formally ended in June 2014. The team produced a poster to represent the most important legacies for the project from the perspective of the project team (Figure 8.1). The most important legacies for the team were able to elucidate, using our approach, were:

- Legacy 1: new ways of thinking and doing – people do new things, or do things differently in their own organisations as a result of the 'Scaling Up Co-Design' project;
- Legacy 2: growing connections – the project created connections or networks between organisations and individuals that otherwise would not have connected, and these lasted beyond the end of the project;
- Legacy 3: cascading co-design – the project's activities and learning on concepts and practice of co-design influenced practices and behaviour beyond the project group or partners.

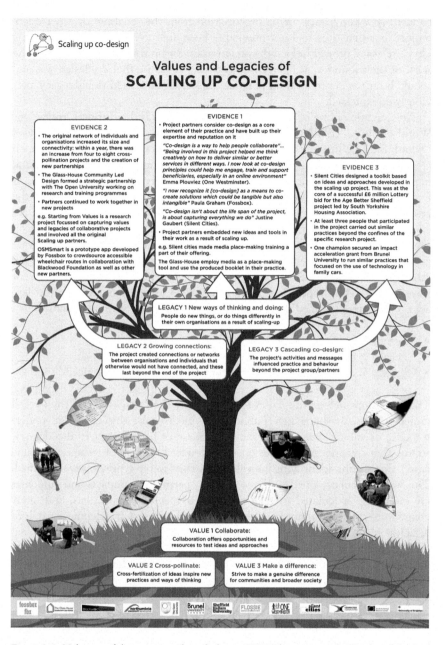

Figure 8.1 Values and legacies as identified in a WeValue process by Scaling Up Co-Design, one of the community organizations who participated in the AHRC 'Starting from Values' project.

Source: poster design by Scaling Up Co-Design (2015). Poster available as free resource, downloadable from: http://empoweringdesignpractices.weebly.com/uploads/1/2/8/5/12856329/scaling_up_values_poster.pdf.

The project also allowed another partner (from the Blackwood Foundation) to identify a key legacy for its organisation from the 'Scaling Up Co-Design' project, but that they had not previously been able to articulate. The 'Scaling Up Co-Design' project helped the organisation regain their connection with the spirit of their founder, Margaret Blackwood, and realise that co-design was and should be at the centre of their practice; thus eliciting an additional legacy, previously unexpressed.

An example of one of the second strand groups was the 'Ethno-Ornithology World Archive' (EWA), a collaborative project involving the University of Oxford, BirdLife International and many other partners worldwide. It focuses on creating and using a web interface to collect information about the cultural importance, uses and symbolism of birds from local communities, and to use it for bird conservation. We worked with members of the EWA team while the project was still in its initial phase. A participatory workshop based on values elicitation and indicator development was used to help the team to reflect on their core values through a participatory workshop. Many different ideas were generated, and again, several clusters of values emerged (Hoover and Harder 2016). In a second workshop, we helped the EWA team to reflect on different ways in which they hoped that their values would be translated into project legacies. The team identified three overarching legacies they wanted to achieve:

- Legacy 1: preservation of knowledge in an accessible format;
- Legacy 2: creation of innovative research methods and practice;
- Legacy 3: establishment of people-centred conservation practice.

The workshops helped the EWA team to clarify their thinking and the overall project vision, to shape new publications and to take this expanded understanding of values forward into the next phase of the project. It also demonstrated that starting from values opens a broader spectrum of legacies. In some cases, this meant identifying new legacies that weren't previously identified. This was particularly the case for community partners, as impacts and outcomes are often not articulated in relation to their specific perspectives, and many community partners do not have the time to reflect on such outcomes or indeed legacies.

If starting from values needs reflection and time, it also requires authenticity and honesty. This is in order to open up space to share what is deeply personal (at an individual but also at a collective level), and make the deeply personal and often intangible 'say-able'. The Authority Research Network (ARN) – our second Strand One group – is an expanding research collective, initiated by a group of doctoral students that engages with questions of authority, positive power, political subjectivity and experience through developing strong social theory and links with practice. They already worked through both collaborative projects and conceptual retreats, as a means to enable reflection and deep interaction. In order to carry out activities for the legacy project, six members of the ARN spent five days on a research retreat in August 2014. Rather than working on a single shared project, this retreat offered an opportunity to work on smaller collaborative projects. With the luxury of five days, the exercise could be divided into several sessions:

1   Initial briefing – introduction to project
2   A walk and talk values elicitation exercise
3   A diagramming values elicitation exercise
4   Using our values-based proto-indicator list
5   Identifying legacies and evidence

Being able to break down the exercise into a number of smaller sessions meant that they could take all necessary time, and could stop and continue if concentration was waning or further discussions were needed. After this process, the legacy project team worked on bringing together evidence and representing ARN's values and key legacies from their collaborative work to date (Hoover and Harder 2016).

In this situation our approach was able to elicit and crystallise values about deeply personal aspects of projects – often central to their participants' motivation and engagement – and to even uncover the conditions for achieving recognized or more authoritative types of impacts. As has been shown in previous chapters, in other contexts, starting from values as an approach also requires careful facilitation and potentially mediation, as it may also open up spaces of tension or conflict. For the Authority Research Group, for example, they had not previously thought about the legitimacy of deeply personal legacies that resulted from their collaborative research projects. But in fact, they established these are indeed crucial to many of their externally recognised academic impacts:

> Actually, these forms of friendship or joy or creativity, are an important part of research. They are essential things to be doing if we want the research we are doing to have the effect we are wanting it to have in society.
>
> (Cardiff University participant, ARN member)

Thus, friendship, for example, shapes how we define ourselves (as academics or community group members), how we build relationships with collaborators, develop projects or supervise others. But it remains a value that is left intangible, unexpressed, and therefore unrecorded and un-evaluated. This means it – like similar values such as trust and integrity – are not taken seriously as both vital components of community-based practices, and an crucial legacy of values-in-action.

The importance of Arts and Humanities approaches

A key finding was that Arts and Humanities approaches are essential in developing a values-based approach to evaluating the legacies of collaborative research projects. This is because, first, they enable people to articulate the detailed meaning of value words, for instance by referring to emotions, narratives, or visually representing rather than just verbally describing these. Second, working from an Arts and Humanities perspective explicitly engages with the articulation of both subjective and inter-subjective values and legacies: this requires different ways of accessing feelings, perceptions and thoughts. Third, it is the Arts and Humanities that can provide a critical lens for examining potential problems of seeking consensus in values –as this can hide power dynamics, or obviate important differences. It should be noted that the SfV team explicitly sought to identify where consensus was or was not present. Finally, in representing these intangible but rich legacies, bullet points or reports alone could not capture the concept of legacies, and specifically show how these were linked to values.

In this study, in particular, we developed the rich visually oriented work already begun around measurement methods with groups like Echeri (as shown in Chapter 3). Here, though, the aim was to both capture and communicate the interwoven intangible legacies for each group, and for the study as a whole. We experimented with different ways in which we could represent legacies, from tables and spreadsheets, to word clouds, illustrations, mind maps, comic strips, video production and illustration. In a 'Rethinking Impact' workshop, for example, we explored using individual and collective drawing as a method of guiding reflection on values, because we'd noticed that people sometimes struggle to find the words to talk about things that matter to them. We wanted to find out whether making images and discussing them together could trigger interesting conversations, and maybe draw out some values that might not have been mentioned otherwise. In doing so, we recognized that 'values' are dynamic. Reflecting, drawing and talking together may actually change people's understanding of what's important to them – as individuals, and/or as groups. This approach was trialled at the pilot session in London as well as the AHRC-organised 2014 Cardiff Festival. Values-based images created by the participants were captured and incorporated into two mixed media canvas panels. A third panel was based on reflections on the sessions, both in written form and as images, and aimed to capture important learning about the collective drawing method itself.

At the end of our study and at a final event, we asked two visualization artists from the group *Endless Possibilities* to do a drawing that represented some of the emerging learning and outcomes from the *Starting from Values* project itself. They visually express a process of generating stories through different values-lenses that can open up both deeply personal and collectively shared intangible values, and can shape these into explicit values-in-action with recognised and important impacts (Figure 8.2). In addition, the StV report (Hoover and Harder 2016) was created in an interactive, non-linear format, with links to external content, as well as to project videos and other resources.

This study concluded that, with care, it seems that using Arts and Humanities approaches, and by starting with values, we can elicit, collect – even take

Figure 8.2 'Starting from Values: Intangible Legacies'. Poster capture of the learning from this AHRC project, as summarized at its final consortium event.

Source: illustration by Karen Smithson and Eleanor Beer/Endless Possibilities, commissioned by the Starting from Values project. Available as a free download from http://arts.brighton.ac.uk/__data/assets/pdf_file/0003/186519/Starting-from-Values_small.pdf.

measures of – more representative intangible legacies that usually get missed out or ignored. We also looked across the legacies from different projects and partners and identified what those legacies could tell us generally about the nature of community-university collaborations. Ultimately two crucial key themes emerged:

- new knowledge, ideas and inspiration linked to the nature of the cross-boundary, interdisciplinary work and;
- friendship, networks and connections that are qualitatively deep and lasting.

Especially the second may seem trivial, but the significance of these aspects should not be underestimated: finding shared ground in collaborative and cross-context research is challenging, and when this happens successfully it is likely because substantial effort and work have been put into building deep and trusting relationships. It is thus important to find appropriate ways of expressing and presenting such legacies. For the community partners the collaborations:

- embedded a new degree of critical thinking within community partners;
- increased their confidence as professionals – e.g. new concepts of language about their work, such as co-design;
- built capacity and inspiration to pass on this to others in the community, beyond project networks;
- enabled the confidence and ability to strategically reposition themselves.

For the academic partners, the co-partnerships:

- brought 'society' to their desks;
- brought new perspectives to their research;
- led to new overall directions to future work;
- influenced other academics, or even institutions similarly, e.g. to value community-university collaborations in teaching and research.

Ultimately, we have found that *legacy* is a productive concept for moving away from 'impact' assessments towards longer-term, complex and explicitly subjective ways of evaluating community–university collaborative research (particularly in the Arts and Humanities). 'Impact' is often defined as the demonstrable contribution that research can make to the economy and society. Here, the researchers' values are usually assumed as unproblematically shared, as are intended outcomes. Legacies, as we noted in the introduction to this chapter, open up values to a range of perspectives and agendas. This reveals tensions and gaps, clarifies what is shared and what not; and generates additional – often intangible – values that would otherwise be ignored. Most crucially, making values explicit can help to authorise multi- and inter-subjective ways of knowing, especially where objective measures are neither relevant nor possible.

Science and social science may have objectively measurable *impacts*, but capturing measures of *legacy* may require arts and humanities approaches by virtue of legacy's embedded multi-subjectivity and values-judgment potential.

Note

1 More details about the Starting from Values project can be found at http://arts. brighton.ac.uk/projects/starting-from-values-evaluating-intangible-legacies. More details about the AHRC Connected Communities work can be found at https:// connected-communities.org/.

References

Facer, K. and Enright, B. (2016). *Creating Living Knowledge: The Connected Communities Programme, community university relationships and the participatory turn in the production of knowledge, Bristol: University of Bristol/AHRC Connected Communities.* Retrieved from https://connected-communities.org/index.php/creating-living-knowledge-report/.

Hoover, Elona and Harder, Marie (2016) *Starting from Values: Evaluating Intangible Legacies Project Report* [Report (for external body) Retrieved from from: http://eprints. brighton.ac.uk/15221/. Accessed 23 April 2018.

9 Towards sustainable behaviour change in schools

The values-based framework explored and developed throughout this book has now been extensively tested in real evaluation contexts across many diverse civil society organizations, spread over three continents (Podger *et al.* 2010, 2013; Harder *et al.* 2014b; Burford *et al.* 2012, 2013a, 2013b, 2015; ESDinds 2011). As already outlined, part of these developments has been to go beyond the original ESDinds Project's aim of creating a values-based evaluation system for CSOs; because our emergent and open-ended approach continually revealed new areas for investigation. One aspect, value-action gaps, briefly covered in Chapter 4, is the focus here. We wanted to explore the complex relationships between value subscription as manifested through *discourse* (what people say) and through overt *action* (what they do); with the critical test of value presence being a consistency between the two. The ultimate aim, then, is not merely more explicit values, or more explicit actions, but an increased, explicit and transparent consistency between individual and group values and actions; that is, real long-term and robust behaviour change. How, then, can organizations reveal their own value-action gaps, as well as developing and testing ways of enabling individual and group behaviour change to close those gaps?

The exploratory study outlined here was undertaken as part of the Partnership for Education and Research about Responsible Living (PERL) project that ran from 2012–2015.[1] The focus was on Education for Sustainable and Responsible Living (EfSRL) teaching in schools, and how this might be better achieved. This was an international project that aimed to inspire students to identify their own values, and recognize and strengthen the skills necessary to ensure they survive and thrive in the 21st century. A workgroup was tasked to use ideas from our values-based approach to develop a framework that might contribute to the identification and closure of value-action gaps within a secondary school context. This was based on the 2013 PERL Work Plan arguing that: 'throughout the decade, most education about sustainable lifestyles has centred around explaining the dire consequences of what has been done wrong' (p. 4).

School curricula generally include scientific information on the state of the planet and its resources, the challenges of climate change, biodiversity conservation, food and water security, pollution control, and other environmental problems, and social science perspectives on the human population, its consumption patterns and social and economic disparities. However, this approach has inherent problems. First, there is a knowledge-action gap when such scientific knowledge is not sufficient to change behaviours. In fact, such approaches are, often conducive to inertia and despair, as people feel that they cannot 'do anything' about such global-scale challenges. Second, motivation and commitment are generally rooted at a deeper level of emotions and values; here formal education should have a responsibility to inculcate the fundamental values of a nation and culture in each new generation of citizens. This is the focus of values-based learning. A third important component is institutional frameworks that can either encourage or impede changes in behaviour.

Thus, in order to stimulate active agency and achieve real change, it is necessary to frame EfSRL in positive and constructive terms (Harder *et al.* 2014a). This may be achieved by co-creating visions of a desirable future, with the need to 'examine and identify the values base from which [these visions] should spring' (PERL 2013: 4). Of course, articulating this values base also requires participants to reflect on value-action gaps. For students and staff, thinking about the future that they would most like to see for their school, in an ideal world, helped to focus their attention on things that mattered to them but may not have been fully enacted in the school at present.

This, in turn, led to an adaptation from our previous approaches. While it would be possible to use our existing approach to work with teachers, based on our values-based indicators iterative process (for example, within their in-service training) a more immediate and appealing design prospect was to adapt our existing values-based framework to create a toolkit that could be used by teachers with students in the classroom. In this way, students in particular would be enabled to clarify and express their values around sustainability and responsible living, as well as any gaps between these values and current actions (both for themselves individually and within the schools' curricula).

Following discussion, the starting point for the project was framed by three pairs of propositions, which collectively constituted a statement of the problematic situations prior to the start of the project and the preferred future situations (Table 9.1). Within the PERL context, this focused on enabling students to feel empowered about making changes towards sustainable and responsible living, and to see what specific actions they could take towards changing behaviours and attitudes; as well as the kinds of methods that could effectively underpin such a behaviour change process.

Selecting values indicators, designing a process

As with other iterations of our values-based framework, we used a series of methods to investigate what were the values specifically relevant for EfSRL teaching in secondary schools. This started from a new analysis of several datasets that we had previously collected during our explorations of values in other educational contexts, a process described in more detail elsewhere (Burford *et al.* 2015). This

Table 9.1 Defining the problem; current and preferred situations in the teaching of Education for Sustainable and Responsible Living (EfSRL)

Problematic situation (at start)	Preferred future situation
1A: Teaching of EfSRL in schools typically focuses on examining current global problems (e.g. climate change) and their likely consequences: may contribute to apathy and despondency.	1B: Teaching of EfSRL in schools focuses on developing values and skills necessary for envisioning and co-creating better futures; contributes towards a sense of power to effect change.
2A: Even when students and teachers do envision 'better futures', they may not recognise where their current actions and behaviours are incongruent with these futures, or take appropriate and effective steps to modify them (i.e. value-action gaps are not identified and closed).	2B: Students and teachers understand where their current actions or behaviours are incongruent with their envisioned 'better futures' (i.e. identify value-action gaps) and take appropriate and effective steps to modify them (i.e. begin to close these gaps).
3A: Although evidence suggests that a values-based indicators toolkit may be helpful in ameliorating problematic situations 1A and 2A, the available toolkit (WeValue) is not fit for purpose because it was developed with and by CSOs in a project evaluation context and its vocabulary reflects the values and priorities of CSOs, albeit with an interest in EfSRL.	3B: A values-based indicators toolkit is developed with and by teachers and students in a secondary school context, such that its vocabulary reflects values and priorities of a positive approach to EfSRL within formal education. The toolkit is effective in transforming problematic situations 1A and 1B into preferred situations 2A and 2B, respectively.

Source: adapted from Burford *et al.* (2015) Making the Invisible Visible: designing Values-Based Indicators and Tools for Identifying and Closing 'Value Action Gaps.' In Didham, R. J., Doyle, D., Klein, J., and Thoresen, V. W. (Eds.) *Responsible Living: Concepts, Education and Future Perspectives.* Berlin Heidelberg: Springer Verlag, p. 113.

led to a reference list of over 300 values statements or triggers (proto-indicators), which was then reviewed by the PERL project workgroup, consisting of seven members with a diverse range of professional roles and experiences in EfSRL. Through an iterative process of selection, clustering and discussion, this was reduced to a shortlist of 38 that were felt to be useful for evaluating schools and 15 that were felt to be helpful for supporting teaching and learning at the classroom level.

Reflection on this shortlist highlighted, however, that it was still not fit for purpose. For example, the key proto-indicator 'Students acquire values and competencies different from those of materialistic, technocratic societies' did not provide sufficient detail about what the desired competencies might actually be. To generate more detailed potential statements researchers worked from a text based on more than 25 years of research in diverse Indigenous societies, *Nature and the Human Soul* by Bill Plotkin (2009). A content analysis of selected chapters of this text was conducted to generate new indicators for review by the workgroup, and 37 of these were added to the 'teaching and learning' shortlist. Additional proto-indicators were also contributed by PERL workgroup members:

some directly, and others through a written survey. After further revisions by workgroup members and three UK secondary school teachers, the final shortlists consisted of 32 proto-indicators for whole-school evaluation and 42 for supporting teaching and learning. In effect, these represented an entirely new derivation of the 'trigger statements' used in the original WeValue toolkit, developed entirely for the specific context of schools.

In principle this represented a large-scale change from many characteristics of the original values-based approaches, and the researchers decided to embrace this fact and follow research through design ideas towards a new goal – to develop a values-approaches toolkit suitable for children to use. At this point, the first priority was to reword some of the indicators to make them more accessible to youth. We also realized that since the focus of the toolkit had shifted towards reflection and learning rather than formal evaluation, it would be more useful to refer to the statements as 'skills for sustainable and responsible living' (SRL) rather than as 'proto-indicators'.

Having shifted focus from teachers to students, the design of the actual activities that would constitute the school's toolkit itself was heavily influenced by Kim Sabo Flores's pioneering work on youth participatory evaluation (Sabo Flores 2008; Hochachka 2005; Seamon and Zajonc 1998). We also drew on Vygotsky's theory that children develop and learn by 'performing a head taller than they are' (Torbert 2001: 102). Sabo Flores highlights the importance of play and performance in youth participatory evaluation, and advocates relating to young people '*as* evaluators, not merely *as if* they were evaluators' (Sabo Flores 2008: 23; Seamon and Zajonc 1998). This subtle but crucial distinction can be understood through the analogy of watching actors in a theatre 'as' their characters, rather than 'as if' they were their characters.

This led ultimately to the design and creation of three separate values-based learning toolkits:

- Measuring what matters: Values-based Indicators (a methods sourcebook).
- Discovering what matters: A Journey of Thinking and Feeling (activities designed with students, for students).
- Growing a Shared Vision: A Toolkit for Schools (activities for organisational and staff development).

So, for example, as the student learning toolkit explains:

> Through the activities in the toolkit, you can understand what your own values are, and how to live by them. You may also find out things about yourself that you want to work on. This toolkit is simple to follow, containing only the information required. It does not need lots of materials or preparation. Any group of students can use it in any setting. The activities in the toolkit will guide you through your own 'journey of thinking and feeling'. They can be adapted to your own language, culture and social, environmental and economic situation.

You can ask a teacher, parent or staff member to facilitate the activities, or some of you can learn to become student facilitators to help everyone to get the best out of the activities. The facilitator should try to link all the things that come out of the activities, so that the questions and ideas raised in the beginning will make sense at the end. A group should be no more than 10 students. If there are more of you, divide into smaller groups with a student facilitator for each.

You will learn to build trust in each other, and to encourage expression and free speech, while respecting each other's privacy. What you all say should go no further than the room.

Some things may require the help of a teacher or administrator. For example, you should ask the school management to agree that you can present your recommendations from activity 8 at the school assembly and to carry out a minimum of three of them. You may need permission to do some activities during school hours, or to use school facilities for artistic creations.

(PERL 2014: 5)

Testing the prototype school's toolkit

Following this initial phase of the project, we set out to train teachers and students in using our prototype school's toolkit. We worked through the toolkit activities with nine 'student governors' (i.e. students who had been elected by their peers as members of the school council) aged between 14 and 17, in two separate sessions at an English secondary school. The sessions with the student governors had two separate aims: testing the newly designed activities, and training these youth as peer facilitators with a view to having them subsequently facilitate activities for younger students (aged 12–13). These exercises also highlighted some new SRL skills, which we added to the provisional 'menu'.

In the first session, we began with the two values elicitation exercises, modified from Sabo Flores (2008) to make them suitable for values elicitation in schools:

a   'The First Thing You Think Of': asking students to write down the first thing that came into their minds when the facilitator mentioned certain words, i.e. 'participation', 'community', 'sustainability', and the name of the school itself (Sabo Flores 2008: 52).
b   'The "Yes, And ..." Game': encouraging students to create a 'collective story' about the type of future they would like to see for their school, in which each new participant had to acknowledge the preceding contribution by saying 'Yes, and ...' (Sabo Flores 2008: 56).

These, and other methods we used or suggested are shown in Table 9.2.

We then introduced the already developed list of indicators for SRL skills and asked the student governors to reflect on the relative importance of the skills to them, first individually (by placing green and red stickers next to those they viewed as most and least important, respectively, on their own copy of the original list) and then collectively (by using wrapped chocolates to 'vote' for their favourites on the large list, with the new skills added). The list of indicators was as follows:

- Taking responsibility for our learning and using our own initiative;
- Having an insight into possible consequences of what we say and do;
- Using our mistakes as starting points for learning and growth;
- Connecting knowledge from different subjects, as a way of thinking about solutions to difficult problems;
- Thinking critically about the ideas and information that are given to us;
- Having the courage to take a step beyond our 'comfort zone';
- Helping people to solve conflicts, by listening to both sides and trying to find acceptable solutions.
- Listening to other people and trying to understand what they really mean;
- Acknowledging and incorporating different points of view (e.g. in our thinking, writing, research);
- Finding the courage to be ourselves;
- Feeling that we have the power to create change and solve problems in our local communities;
- Remembering to use non-violent communication in tense situations (e.g. using 'I feel' statements rather than blaming others);
- Finding or creating safe spaces to express our emotions (e.g. nature, art, music, friendship groups, sports);
- Applying our subject knowledge and skills to understanding problems in our local communities (schools/families/neighbourhoods etc.);
- Thinking about what we buy and what we throw away, remembering that future generations will depend on the same natural resources as we do now;
- Resisting the pressure (e.g. from advertisers) to buy things we don't really need;
- Caring for our environment – especially endangered species and ecosystems, injured or unwanted wildlife, and damaged habitats;
- Learning to be comfortable with who we are;
- Having a strong sense of belonging in nature;
- Developing our own personal style by getting to know interests, attitudes and sensitivities;
- Thinking of ways to reduce waste, carbon emissions and pollution;
- Evaluating what's important to us and what isn't;
- Looking after ourselves and our families;
- Communicating face to face, spending quality time with people;
- Accepting others instead of judging them;
- Choosing jobs that we love, not just thinking about how much we can earn.

Table 9.2 List of activities for measuring and reflecting on SRL skills

Activity 1	*Silent Catch*
Goals	To help us to relax and bond. To use non-verbal communication and begin to discover some of our skills. To introduce a reflective mindset.
Description	We throw a ball to each other at random in silence for a certain amount of time. We try to keep the ball in play by making an eye-contact. After a while, another ball can be thrown in to add challenge and fun to the game. No one goes out if they don't catch the ball. The play continues until the facilitator ends it.
Required materials	A small ball or anything that can be thrown, preferably soft.
Preparation	Clear a space to play.
Approximate time needed	5–10 minutes.
Facilitation tips	Encourage the use of non-verbal communication. In the most successful cases, the members of the group are often very comfortable with silence – treating it not as a warning sign that people are not participating enough, but as a space in which the 'inner voice' can be heard.
Reflection	Understanding the experiences: 'What happened?' How did you feel during the activity? Recognizing skills: What skills did you use during the game? How did you communicate with others? Relating it to real life: How would the skills that you used here be useful in your life?
Activity 2	*The first thing you think of when I say …'*
Goals	To set us on the path of thinking about ourselves and our future. We create our own individual understanding of our immediate environment and explore together what it means.
Description	Each category is read out loud one at a time. Each of us writes the first thing that comes into our head on a small piece of paper. Our answers can be placed on a table and stuck on a large piece of paper (one per category). Categories: [Name of our School/Group/Project, etc.] Social Life Sustainability Participation Hopes for the future
Required materials	1 large piece of paper for each category (e.g. flip chart page) 5 small pieces of paper (e.g. Post-it® notes) for each student Pens for everyone

Preparation	Write the name of each category in the middle of a large paper and divide out pens and small papers for each student.
Approximate time needed	30 minutes.
Facilitation tips	Encourage the participants to write whatever comes into their mind. It can be a thought, a feeling, a question or 'I don't know', good or bad. It is not so important what the students write on their small papers: what goes on in their minds matters. If you see any inappropriate words on the small papers, let them be there but ignore them. Focus on the serious ones.
Reflection	Understanding the experiences: How did you feel when trying to write a reaction to each category? Recognizing skills: What skills did you use during this activity by yourself? and with others? Relating it to real life: What did you learn from this experience? What does it tell you about the meaning of these things in your life?

Activity 3

	The Future We Want (The 'Yes, And …' game).
Goals	To help us think about the future we want and then verbalise our vision for others. By agreeing to accept the previous hope, we create a space where we know our own hopes will be accepted.
Description	We each think of our hopes for the future. Someone starts by saying: 'In the future I hope to see …' and add their own hope to the sentence. Each person takes a turn to say 'yes' to accept the sentence said by the preceding person, then 'and' before adding their own hope. Go round the group twice.
Required materials	One big sheet of paper, and separate strips of paper (two per student), to write down the hopes. Two marker pens.
Preparation	Arrange the room so that everyone can sit in one large circle. Choose one person to write down all the hopes on the large paper, and another to write each hope on a separate strip of paper.
Approximate time needed	15–20 minutes.
Facilitation tips	This can be done at an organizational level (e.g. hopes for the future of your school/group/project, etc.) or at the level of wider society, or both. Each student needs to be asked to listen to the other students before saying their own sentence. The point is to support each other and acknowledge different kinds of hopes. Make sure the rule is to accept others' contribution even if they don't agree. If they disagree with the hope mentioned before them, ask them to think about whether they can add another element to the story to make it more acceptable to them.

continued

Table 9.2 Continued

Reflection	Understanding the experiences • What happened? • Were you working together? Recognizing skills • What skills did you use during this activity by yourself? • and with others? Relating it to real life • Are these realistic hopes? • What skills do you need to make these a reality?
Activity 4 Goals	*Indicators of skills and values* To focus on the skills and values we need to live a sustainable and responsible life. To discover we already have some of the skills needed to create the future we want. To get a holistic approach to living a responsible life by finding connections between indicators.
Description	1) Individually The indicator list (see Appendix) is introduced as ideas that are important for some people. Ask everyone to read and think about how they feel about the indicators, marking the five most important ones with a ✓ and the five least important ones with a ✗. There are no right or wrong answers. 2) Collectively We gather around a large size list of indicators on a table. We place sweets/tokens on our own choices of most important ones (one for each indicator). We discuss together and decide collectively five most important ones. We can move the sweets/tokens if we change our minds and can add new indicators by writing in the blank spaces. 3) Clustering Cut the indicators (large font versions from Annex 2) into separate strips and group them. This allows us to make sense of our own connections instead of seeing the indicators as an isolated list of sentences. We can make our own rules about how to group them, and whether to bring in some or all of our own values-based indicators ('hopes for the future') from Activity 3 as well.
Required materials	Copies of the indicator list (see Appendix) for everyone, and pens. One large size indicator list. One set of indicator strips, cut up (Annex 2). Enough sweets/tokens for the collective part of the activity.
Preparation	Copy the indicator list for everyone and create one large size list. (If you don't have access to poster printing facilities, you can write out the indicators by hand – they don't all have to fit on one page). Get the sweets/tokens and clear the space for the collective work.

Approximate time needed	40 minutes.
Facilitation tips	Encourage discussion throughout the activity of all the skills that the students currently possess, and how they can use them.
Reflection	Understanding the experiences

- Which were your most important values?
  - Have they changed? Why?
  - How was it to work with others?
- Recognizing skills
  - Did you use any of the skills while doing the exercise? Relating it to real life
  - Did you know you have this many skills already?
  - How does that make you feel?
  - In what kind of situations can you practice these skills?

Activity 5	
Goals	*Spatial survey* To help us to evaluate where we think our school (or group, project, etc.) is now, in relation to each of our three most important indicators.
Description	1) Prioritizing We choose our three most important indicators (these can be the 'hopes for the future' from Activity 3, and/or the printed indicators from Activity 4). Write each of the chosen indicators on a piece of paper. 2) Measuring The three pieces of paper representing the most important indicators are stuck on the wall at one end of the classroom. Students all start from the opposite wall, marking the 'not at all' point, and move to the mark where they feel their school is at. Repeat this for each indicator.
Required materials	Pieces of paper saying 'Not at all', 'a little', 'adequate', 'good', 'excellent'.
Preparation	Measure by eye the halfway point of the classroom or hall, and place the 'adequate', then place the markers for 'a little' and 'good' half way to each end. Opposite ends of the room form the 'not at all' and 'excellent' (see room plan below).
Approximate time needed	20 minutes.
Facilitation tips	Ask the students to go with what they really feel and ignore where the others stand. They can stand in between the markers if they want to.

continued

Table 9.2 Continued

Reflection	Understanding the experiences • What happened here? • How did you choose the three most important indicators? • Were you able to think for yourself? • To what degree did you hide your real belief once you saw where others had chosen to stand? • What does this tell you?

Layout of the classroom or hall for Activity 5 (Spatial Survey)

Stick the marker for 'not at all' on the wall at this end of the room. Students start here. If they feel the indicator is not being lived out at all, they stand still and don't move forward.

Place the marker for 'a little' on the floor here. Students move to this point if they feel the indicator is only being lived out a little in the school.

Stick the marker for 'adequate' on the floor here. Students move to this point if they feel the indicator is being lived out adequately.

Stick the marker for 'good' on the floor here. Students move to this point if they feel the indicator is being lived out well.

Stick the marker for 'excellent', and the indicator, on the wall here. Students stand next to the indicator if they feel it is being lived out as well as it could be.

Activity 6	
Goals	*Art week* To take a week to internalize and vocalize our thoughts and feelings on the process so far.
Description	We can do this in school if our teacher agrees, and our own time if we want to. We go outside and find our own quiet place in nature, turn off our cell-phones, and open up to observe by using different senses. We capture the feelings that emerge by writing in our own journal or writing ourselves a letter, or we can express our thoughts through drama, dance, video, painting, writing or making a collection of song lyrics that have meaning for us, as well as engaging online.
Required materials	Physical space to showcase their visible journey or art expressions (e.g. in the school halls), or to show to others such as parents if they wish. Ensure that suitable materials are available when needed
Approximate time needed	A week
Facilitation tips	It might be helpful to check in half-way through the week and share ideas (this is optional).
Reflection (one week later)	Understanding the experiences • What did you think, see, listen and do during the week? • How did these things help you process the activities? • What motivated you to take part in the week?

Activity 7

Goals
Role play: 'Living' our values and skills
To practice using the skills we need for our hopes to become a reality.

Description
Groups of 3–4 students create a role play about one hope from Activity 3, or indicator of a skill from Activity 4, and present it to the other groups.

Required materials
None required

Preparation
Have the hopes for the future (from Activity 3) and the three most important indicators (from Activity 5) visible.

Approximate time needed
40 minutes

Facilitation tips
Help each group to involve everyone rather equally. Do not encourage showing off.

Reflection
Understanding the experiences
- What happened?
- Did you feel you were able to express your hopes?

Recognising skills
- What skills did you use doing this activity?

Relating it to real life
- What did you learn about communicating your hopes to others?
- What other ways are there to express your hopes?

Activity 8

Goals
Our messages to the school
To enable us to discover the power of our 'voice' and communicate our improved vision of school life.

Description
We come up with ideas for what our hopes would look like in practice in school. We think of at least six recommendations for the school management. We also think about things that we and our peers can do in order to make our vision a reality. We prepare for presenting our recommendations at the school assembly.

Required materials
Whatever the students feel is necessary

Preparation
Whatever the students feel is necessary

Approximate time needed
Variable

Facilitation tips
Before starting this activity, make sure that the school management is committed to putting at least three of the students' recommendations into practice, and giving them regular feedback on what is being done and what the next steps will be. If the students come up with powerful 'messages to the school' but these are not seen to be acted upon, disappointment and frustration will result.
If you are doing this activity in a non-school setting such as a youth group, think creatively about how to frame it before you start – e.g. do you want to send 'messages to the director', or maybe 'messages to the local government'?

continued

Table 9.2 Continued

Reflection (after presenting the recommendations at the school assembly)	Understanding the experiences • What happened? Recognising skills • What skills did you use doing this activity? Relating it to real life • How can you carry all this learning with you and use it from now on?

Source: reprinted from PERL Toolkit (2014) *Discovering What Matters: A Journey of Thinking and Feeling.* ESDinds Team, Values and Sustainability Research Group, University of Brighton for PERL.

The activities were well received, although the collective story was challenging for some students, and there were several awkward silences. In discussing the SRL skills list, it became evident that many of these are skills that students have already learned – often through arts, sports and other extra-curricular activities, as well as from their core curriculum – but may not necessarily have articulated before.

Further activities were carried out in the second session, The facilitation capacity-building aspect was challenging to explain, however, and created confusion – until one of the student governors realised that we wanted them to 'be us' – i.e. take on our own roles. In retrospect, it might have been helpful to work through all the activities once first, before separately focusing on the elements of good facilitation and allowing the students to practice facilitating each other.

Identification and closure of value-action gaps: some preliminary reflections

The school toolkit activities were well received by the student governors during the capacity building sessions, and generated some lively, and generally positive, discussions. In the first session, the collective story of 'the future we want' generated a number of new SRL skill statements that were not present in either the original WeValue list (see Appendix) or the reference list developed specifically for this project. These included, among others:

- Evaluating what's important to us and what isn't;
- Looking after ourselves and our families;
- Not being so dependent on technology that we lose the ability to write and socialize (communicating face to face; spending quality time with people);
- Accepting others instead of judging them;
- Choosing jobs that we love instead of only thinking about how much we can earn.

Crucially this exercise, by its very nature, required participants to reflect on value-action gaps. It led to some important realisations about how different SRL skills are interconnected, and a revaluing of some statements that had initially been seen as unimportant.

The 'human survey'/spatial survey (see Table 9.2) seems to be another helpful tool for assessing values enactment and highlighting value-action gaps, and an important observation was that consensus among students is not necessary in order for the exercise to be useful. On one of the three chosen skills, 'Maintain a sustainable society, e.g. recycling, energy', there was a strong consensus that the school was not doing enough and that these issues should be taken more seriously by the senior management. On the others, however ('Be less judgemental – accept people more' and 'Not to become so dependent on technology that we lose the ability to write and socialize'), there was a wide spread of responses – ranging, in the latter case, from around 10 per cent to

80 per cent agreement. This prompted lively discussions, which resulted in some students changing their positions in the 'survey'.

Finally, the approach of role-play proved very powerful, enabling students to embody the two contrasting situations of judgement and acceptance. Perhaps understandably, students spent more time enacting well-known problems than envisioning workable solutions, and we realised that the activity guidelines could be reworded to encourage future facilitators to focus on the positive. Nonetheless, participants understood the point of the exercise and contributed meaningfully to a follow-up discussion about what could be done differently. While some suggested that the senior management should take a tougher stance on bullying, others acknowledged that they themselves – as peer leaders – could play a role in helping to create a climate where everyone feels accepted and valued.

We envisage that these processes of identifying and closing value-action gaps could be taken further, e.g. by asking students to reflect on their chosen SRL skills through arts-based activities (painting, poetry, music, dance, monologue, etc.) and then to identify specific, measurable actions that they can take themselves and/or request the senior management team to implement. The senior management, in return, might pledge to implement a minimum number (e.g. three) of the viable suggestions made by the youth for building a better future at the school. In this respect, the willingness of senior management to listen to students and implement their viable suggestions is crucial, as it could be profoundly empowering for the youth to see their work leading to observable changes within the school. In this case study, teaching staff were only minimally involved, which could have limited its impact.

Concluding thoughts on the school's toolkit

> Your education should help you learn to live responsibly and sustainably. You should try to become responsible citizens, respectful of society, the planet and its boundaries. For this you need to think critically about world problems and to decide to adopt lifestyles and consumption patterns that are:
>
> • environmentally responsible, respecting the need for our civilization to remain within planetary environmental boundaries; and
> • socially responsible, contributing to social justice with a fair and sustainable distribution of the limited resources available to the world population, while preserving the planet's capacity to support future generations.
>
> In school you learn scientific knowledge and intellectual understanding, but these are often not enough for you to want to change your behaviour and lifestyle. Before you want to do something and decide to do it, you need to feel strongly about it, and that will reflect your values. By becoming

aware of your values, discovering your skills and sharing your views with each other, you will be better able to live a responsible and sustainable life.

(PERL 2014, 4)

The aim of this project was to move students and staff towards understanding how to improve sustainable behaviours both as individuals and within school curricula. Crucially, this needed to be built on a values-based approach. Our exploratory study showed that each of the 'problematic situations' outlined in Table 9.1 at the beginning of this chapter was beginning to shift towards its respective 'preferred situation' in our case study examples – albeit to a limited extent. We could see that the toolkit was valuable in revealing value-action gaps, but not yet really operating to close those gaps. We suggest that this demonstrates that it is possible, on a small scale and with an amenable group of students, to adopt a positive and constructive approach to the teaching of EfSRL, which focuses on developing values and skills necessary for envisioning and co-creating better futures; that can identify value-action gaps, and at least begin to understand how they might be closed.

In the process, we learnt how important it was to elicit values statements from young people in their own words, as a process based on analysis of what is important to teachers may not capture everything that matters to students. The combination of an explicit values elicitation step with reflection on a pre-existing 'menu' can ensure that participants are both empowered to express whatever is already important to them, and challenged with new ideas that they might not previously have thought about. In addition, we learned that the students felt they were *already* practising many of the skills described in the list, often outside the core curriculum; but they had neither articulated them in words, nor previously thought of them as 'skills for sustainable and responsible living'. This can be related to comments by teachers that several of the skills in the proto-indicators reference list were barely covered in (or even, in a few cases, were entirely absent from) the UK national secondary curriculum. Merely by introducing them as topics of conversation, and linking them explicitly to SRL, the toolkit has already contributed towards the closure of value-discourse gaps. And whilst our small and prototyping study could not close value-action gaps around behaviour change towards sustainable and responsible living, it does illuminate where these gaps occur, and what kinds of processes within schools could lead to more robust behaviour change.

Note

1 PERL is a partnership of educators and researchers from over 140 institutions in more than 50 countries working to empower citizens to live responsible and sustainable lifestyles. The project was funded by the European Community, Norwegian Ministry of Children, Equality and Social Inclusion, Hedmark University College Norway. For more details on the University of Brighton-based element of this project, go to www.brighton.ac.uk.research-and-enterprise/groups/values-and-sustainability/perl.aspx.

References

Burford, G., Hoover, E., Dahl, A., and Harder, M. K. (2015) 'Making the Invisible Visible: Designing Values-Based Indicators and Tools for Identifying and Closing "Value Action Gaps"'. In Didham, R. J., Doyle, D., Klein, J., Thoresen, V. W. (Eds.) *Responsible Living: Concepts, Education and Future Perspectives* (pp. 113–134). Berlin, Heidelberg: Springer Verlag.

Burford, G., Hoover, E., Velasco, I., Janouskova, S., Jimenez, A., Piggot, G., Podger, D., and Harder, M. K. (2013a) 'Bringing the "Missing Pillar" into Sustainable Development Goals: Towards Intersubjective Values-Based Indicators', *Sustainability*, 5, pp. 3035–3059.

Burford, G., Kissmann, S., Rosado-May, F. J., Alvarado Dzul, S. H., and Harder, M. K. (2012) 'Indigenous Participation in Intercultural Education: Learning from Mexico and Tanzania', *Ecology and Society*, 17(4), p. 33.

Burford, G., Velasco, I., Janouskova, S., Zahradnik, M., Hak, T., Podger, D., Piggot, G., and Harder, M. K. (2013b) 'Field Trials of a Novel Toolkit for Evaluating "Intangible" Values-Related Dimensions of Projects', *Evaluation and Program Planning*, 36(1), pp. 1–14.

ESDinds (2011) *ESDinds: The development of values-based indicators and assessment tools for civil society organizations promoting education for sustainable development. Deliverable 17: Final project report to European Commission Seventh Framework Programme (FP7/2007–2013)*, www.esdinds.eu. ESDinds Project Consortium led by University of Brighton, Brighton.

Harder, M. K., Burford, G., and Hoover, E. (2014a) From 'Sustainable Production' to 'Production as Sustainability': The Emergence of Values-Focused Evaluation. In *Global Research Forum on Sustainable Production and Consumption*, Shanghai, China, Fudan University, Shanghai.

Harder, M. K., Velasco, I., Burford, G., Podger, D., Janouskova, S., Piggot, G., and Hoover, E. (2014b) 'Reconceptualizing "Efffectiveness" in Environmental Projects: Can We Measure Values-Related Achievements?' *Journal of Environmental Management*, 139, pp. 120–134.

Hochachka, G. (2005) *Developing sustainability, Developing the Self: An Integral Approach to Individual and Community Development*. Polis Project, Victoria, Canada.

PERL (2013) *PERL2 Workplan*. The Partnership for Education and Responsible Living. Retrieved from www.perlprojects.org/perl-workplan.html.

PERL (2014) *Discovering What Matters: A Journey of Thinking and Feeling PERL*. Retrieved from http://iefworld.org/fl/PERL_toolkit2.pdf.

Plotkin, B. (2009) *Nature and the Human Soul: Cultivating Wholeness and Community in a Fragmented World*. Novato, CA: New World Library.

Podger, D., Piggot, G., Zahradnik, M., Janouskova, S., Velasco, I., Hak, T., Dahl, A., Jimenez, A., and Harder, M. K. (2010) 'The Earth Charter and the ESDinds Initiative: Developing Indicators and Assessment Tools for Civil Society Organisations to Examine the Values Dimensions of Sustainability Projects', *Journal of Education for Sustainable Development*, 4(2), pp. 297–305.

Podger, D., Velasco, I., Amezcua Luna, C., Burford, G., and Harder, M. K. (2013) 'Can Values Be Measured? Significant Contributions from a Small Civil Society Organisation Through Action Research Evaluation', *Action Research*, 11(1), pp. 8–30.

Sabo Flores, K. (2008) *Youth Participatory Evaluation*. San Francisco, CA: Jossey Bass.

Seamon, D. and Zajonc, A. (1998) *Goethe's Way of Science: A Phenomenology of Nature*. Albany, NY: SUNY.

Torbert, W. (2001) The Practice of Action Inquiry. In Reason, P. and Bradbury, H. (Eds.) *Handbook of Action Research* (pp. 250–260). London: Sage.

Conclusion
What happens when values are central

So where do these apparently diverse and divergent strands of explorations of intangible values approaches take us? Can we see any order in the almost overwhelming amount of different learning, and pathways to learning, that seemed to have sprouted out of the original 'wicked problem' – how to measure intangible shared values? For us, there is order. All the learning acquired has resulted from careful attendance to shoots and offshoots of the original objective: 'How can we help civil society groups find a way to measure and communicate the achievements that are of worth to them?' Without a preconception of what the solution would look like, without a bias for specific disciplinary approaches and accompanying frameworks – in true research through design spirit – we moved only 'towards a better situation' via iteratively reflecting, consulting with partners, exploring in practice, and observing linked findings – and always being guided by the uncompromising need for our work to be considered valid to the CSOs, and to embed artefacts of that validity where possible.

This honest, and conceptually but not methodologically fixed approach, meant that we had to pursue offshoots until we understood enough about their relevance to the main stem of research: a way to measure and communicate locally valid manifestations of value. And the final result was not then one narrowly defined output contributing to an artificially, academically contextualized area of formalized knowledge, but rather a new, problem-focused, practice-based area of knowledge with multiply identified complex interfaces with multiple formal systems of knowledge, roads marked for future journeys. What we ended up with is, indeed, a way to measure manifestations of 'worth' to civil society organisations and other groups concerned to better articulate their own intangible social values. But in order to get there we found that we were revealing relevant but previously hidden, rich and formal research areas about the:

- crystallization of shared values and shared knowledge;
- critical contribution of different types of participation to many processes and the need for a systemized way of studying it;
- inadequacy of current formalized concepts of values to build up a picture of shared values, and some understanding of how to advance that;

- transformational and sometimes emancipatory effects on groups when they can suddenly articulate their intangible values in real terms;
- and the connection of all of this learning towards a future world where values measures can take their place alongside measures of finance and power.

In this chapter, we remind the reader how these strands were carefully nurtured from the original project until their direction was clear and relevance understood. And then we will draw them together to show how they seem to form a new platform of knowledge and an agenda for future research through design, centred on systematic but also open-ended approaches to resolving complex and wicked problems. We also want, finally, to return to one of the original foci of the ESDinds EU-funded project – education for sustainable development – to show how our project has contributed to a deeper conceptualization of the process of social transformation towards sustainability; and of the vital importance of enabling civil society organisations and groups to be able to explicitly articulate, robustly measure and effectively communicate their own intangible but deeply shared values.

The twin functions of measurement and transformation

Early field trials of the ESDinds/WeValue approach highlighted that it is more than just a way to develop measures for a 'project evaluation toolkit', and that it can fulfil several other functions than those for which it was originally designed. But the most major of these was definitely individual and organizational transformation. These two functions of the final values-based system are so closely intertwined, that even when only one is the focus, the other seems to occur regardless. That is, groups focusing on producing measures and evaluation frameworks must first agree concise indicators, and in so doing will go through a collective realization of something they share – particular intangible social values. This very recognition appears to cause collective self-realisation and transformation, and all the nuanced processes leading up to this deserve far more research. Transformative learning is, after all, the golden fleece of many disciplines such as education for sustainable development, and organizational change: and here we have it as a kind of by-product. Similarly, those groups which want to focus on organizational change e.g. by planning more time on the negotiation of their shared values as a group, in great depth (even if they have no particular interest in developing measures for themselves and who might even eschew evaluation) will discover that once their shared values are articulated and laid bare that they will immediately wish to re-prioritise and revise their plans. A de facto evaluation will therefore have taken place. In fact, this effect can be so strong that any group originally thinking of producing measures might stop there, and feel their targets for monitoring are now so obvious that they don't need specific measures in order for the organization to learn more. The facilitated construction of shared values statements one by one, and the laying of these down into a framework which illustrates how they are linked to each other, can influence the group members to adopt behaviours that truly reflect their values – rather than behaviours driven by habit, imitation of others, or their personal self-enhancement values such as desire for wealth and social recognition. Espoused values pale in comparison with the now vivid shared values they have just affirmed with each other, with illustrations from real actions. Bearing in mind these twin functions of measurement and trans-formation that are both useful for CSOs and entry-points for multiple new strands of academic research, we conclude this book by relating below various points of learning along the way to developing and understanding them.

Learning lessons about values-based approaches

This project did not start with any existing values framework, but instead developed one empirically in the field. This grounded, action research, approach was later understood to be absolutely key to the success of the work. Of course researchers cannot be empty vessels, and indeed ours were aware of concepts from different disciplinary frameworks before we set out, but we kept those as background knowledge and were prepared to identify new concepts. Even the concept of 'a value' was not set until we heard how these were described in the field (and as already described, these ended up as illustrative 'indicator' state-ments, not values concepts such as Trust or Equality). In the early work, eight different civil society organizations, of different types and active all over the world, were asked questions to elicit their values and related statements. For example, 'Think of a recent project that you consider had some really good aspects to it. What were those characteristics? Why are they important to you?' Discourse analysis was also carried out on key documents of these CSOs. The values statements and overarching human values evident in this data were drawn out by the researchers, and then checked with the participants for 'face' validity (i.e. did the participants recognise our interpretation as something coming from them). A small, manageable subset of these values was chosen to take forward, and indicators for them that had already been suggested in the interviews were noted, as well as a small number from ethics-based literature. As previously described in more detail, these lists of indicators for each value were taken back to the participants to check their validity. The final list of values and their associated indicators were then taken to ground-level projects in the field to determine if they were useful, relevant and measurable.

In the field it was found that presentation of the values had some use and generated good discussions. However, the pooled lists of indicators (values-based) was found to be very much more – tremendously – useful, almost uni-versal, and very welcomed by the CSOs. The fact that the indicators were so specific, compared to the values that had multiple nuances, meant that groups had little difficulty agreeing which were important to them, and which they wanted to be able to measure. In the end it was found much more effective to skip explorations of values and go straight to the reference list of indicators, which everyone found easy to use and relate to (for a set of example sustainable development indicators, see Appendix). Later work showed that once a group agreed on a subset of the indicators that were important to it, they had little difficulty in articulating which values these represented. A first key lesson learned here was that for discourse purposes the language of the indicators is very much easier to use than that of values underlying them.

Originally it was thought that the indicators would have to be very precisely and rigidly defined in order to be useful, e.g. in allowing comparisons across organisations. However, the fieldwork clearly showed that the CSOs needed to be able to slightly modify the wording of the indicators to feel comfortable using them – and then they were very comfortable. In the end this was seen as a strength rather than a weakness, and a system could still be devised which remained a framework but also allowed some flexibility in interpretation of individual indicators. Thus, a second key lesson learned was that some localisation of the indicators needed to be permitted.

Once CSOs had identified three to six indicators they would like to be able to measure, they were assisted to develop assessment tools that were consistent with the culture and resources of their group. Some preferred questionnaires or interviews; others very creative methods such as painting activities, drama or word elicitation. This localisation of assessment methods was key to the CSOs' acceptance and ownership of the measurement part of the process. The assessment taking place was not an external process applied *to* them, but one which they developed *themselves*. The results were in a form laden with meaning for them, expressing outcomes that were close to their hearts; suddenly they could see tangible assessments that informed not only their group but their supporters and funders of previously intangible outcomes. A third lesson learned here is that *localisation of assessment methods* is key to local ownership, and results in considerably deeper participatory engagement and enthusiasm.

Moreover, in the process of developing their localised assessment methods, CSOs had to explore and deepen their understanding of their own values and manifestations of them in various activities. Because this inherently involved more than one person, the end result was a much firmer group understanding and agreement on these, in real, visible terms throughout their operations. Inevitably what followed was that because the group now had a crystallised and shared vision, they considered how to increase the alignment of their (previously un-crystallized) values with the group behaviours and outcomes – a closing of the values-behaviour gap. A fourth lesson learned is that in the 'doing' the CSOs deepened their 'knowing' of their own aims, and this fed back in to the 'doing'. A fifth lesson is that the groups learned how to measure for themselves; after taking the time to develop their own assessment methods and apply them, it was found that even months later they were applying similar forms of logical thinking to different aspects of their work – they had developed a new transferable skill.

Some of the CSOs then reported back to their funders on their new indicators – for example, about empowerment, emotional connection to nature, opportunities for everyone to have a voice, and the active elicitation of minority views. Funders were surprised to learn these activities were taking place and even now being assessed; some funders then reciprocated by indicating they would be willing to support further activities focused in these newly highlighted areas. A new shared vocabulary between the funders and CSOs had been set up; both could now articulate more precisely which values-based activities were of interest. A sixth lesson learned here is that once a simple framework (such as our reference list of values-based indicators) is used to draw out and crystallize our values, its vocabulary can quickly become useful for wider communication. This was *not true* for the values vocabulary, we started with, which was generally too non-specific and abstract for effective communication.

The most exciting finding of our project, though, is its transformative potential. As already suggested, along the way of undertaking a values-based approach, something extra happens beyond any simple evaluation process; each CSO goes through a significant shift in their thinking. When the participating CSOs first look at the reference list of indicators, they have in mind already what things are important to them. Because that list has itself been drawn from other CSOs who are also values-based, the language and content are very comfortable to the CSOs reading the list, and they relate easily and strongly to the indicators and are able to quickly identify ones matching those important to them. But then we have what the research team has come to call the 'Haagen-Dazs Effect'. The CSO has come to the list with its own choice of favourite indicator in mind, and is searching for it on the list. This favourite indicator comes from the limited, somewhat isolated conversations that CSO has had within its own group, using the limited vocabulary around values that society currently has. It is rather like someone coming to an ice-cream parlour thinking chocolate or vanilla is their favourite flavour, because they have not been exposed to much else. But the proto-indicators list contains a rich variety of value statements drawn from many CSOs – some that the participating CSO had never considered before. It is like seeing, in the ice-cream parlour, a large choice of flavours never before considered; it is not surprising that suddenly something like 'passion fruit sorbet' seems a better representation of 'my favourite'. Similarly, the participating CSO usually finds that some other values-based indicators are much more representative of what is important to them, and, in continuing through the list, goes through a series of steps of self-realization.

By the end, most CSOs end up with a significantly modified list of what indicators are important to them. When more than one person from a CSO does the same, the two compare notes and in so doing learn a great deal about what is important to them jointly. During this discussion they draw out and crystallize what indicators – and thus values – are important to them. What has occurred is a 'transformational learning' event of the highest quality – something organizational change specialists and educators often try to design and implement in vain. It is highly valuable for many reasons, not least for its effect of crystallizing a joint vision drawn out from values-frames of individuals which were probably lying below conscious level – even beyond 'deep frames'. A seventh lesson learned, then, is that there is a values-discourse gap, i.e. between what values people hold and what they can articulate, yet it only takes a brief event with the right mechanisms and process to draw out those values into a shared vocabulary. There are several consulting companies which currently try to trigger such transformational learning events through discussions of values, e.g. to develop mission statements – but those discussions are known for their hours of going around in circles trying to agree on the meaning of words. It seems that this project has unwittingly found a process that is very much more effective and only takes about two hours to produce significant change: through use of the reference list of indicators, drawn from values from similar organizations. We posit that for application in other domains (for example, health or welfare) it would be necessary to derive a new list from relevant organisations in that field. The new list would probably not be very different from the existing one, but is likely to contain some crucial new indicators of specific interest to that domain. An eighth lesson proposed is that the existing list will probably not work beyond the fields it was drawn from (CSOs, sustainable education, ethics-orientated businesses) but the method of producing one can be used to derive new or adapted lists. Work still needs to be done in order to address the challenges of understanding the relevance of the values-based indicators developed in the ESDinds project in different contexts. Indeed, the ESDinds Consortium has found it challenging so far to include a faith-based organisation in the field-testing phase. At an intermediate stage the consortium identified, with insight from the Alliance for Religions and Conservation (ARC) that many faith-based organizations work on long-term timescales that do not fit with those of a two-year research project. This was important for the project consortium, suggesting that future projects which seek to involve faith-based groups should incorporate this into planning and implementation measures, perhaps involving an organization from the outset to enable a more longitudinal engagement.

The final set of lessons we learnt were about what forms of participation are required to enable deep engagement and therefore effective transformative learning for individuals and organizations. As we became more familiar with common results from the workshop approaches, we began to discern that these were greater and lesser depending on some details or conditions. In the end, we identified at least three conditions that appeared to be necessary for good workshop results (transformation and/or production of useful indicators). The first of these is a *functional working group* – a group of people who are already interacting with one another in the context of a specific activity – rather than a diffuse and ill-defined group of individuals, with little in common beyond their interest in values. The second is *meaningful participation by appropriate stakeholders*. What this means is that the roles of different groups of people – directors, managers, staff, volunteers, beneficiaries, etc., – in our values-based system must be congruent with the nature of the hoped-for change. It would be equally unrealistic to expect the senior management team of a CSO to effect a transformation in the way in which the members of its youth group interact with one another, without involving these young people in the process, as to imagine that the youth could transform the organization's investment policy or five-year strategic plan without consulting the management. Third, the success of the exercise is dependent on the existence of *conducive interpersonal processes* within the targeted working group, with or without an external facilitator. By 'conducive interpersonal processes' is meant that groups actually act in accordance with many of the values-in-action statements being discussed. This is true across all the indicators, but in particular, is about those that relate to interacting in a courteous, respectful, open and honest way. As our project progressed, it became clear that joint historical work together, meaningful participation of different team members, and conducive interpersonal processes might be key and even critical to success, and these each deserve more focused research in the future.

Learning lessons for research through design

While participatory action research and co-design may provide the 'how' of systematising research through design (RtD) to facilitate design-centred post-disciplinary work, we can look to the conversation on sustainability and new design knowledge to provide the 'why'. As highlighted by Manzini (2010) societal transformations (he looks specifically at sustainability innovations) cannot and will not be achieved merely by finding better ways to do the things that we have always done. They demand radically new mindsets, and novel approaches to both design and research. Manzini further notes that 'traditional' forms of design knowledge accumulated by professional designers are no longer enough, and that contemporary design processes are increasingly distributed between numerous actors, both with and without formal design training. Thus, breaking down the artificial barriers that separate different forms of knowledge and practice – both between and beyond academic disciplines – through systematic RtD may prove to be a critically important strategy in the global quest for sustainable design solutions.

A caveat to the above discussions is that there are challenges inherent in systematising RtD, which should not be underestimated. As we have noted in this book, the core of a post-disciplinary research agenda is defined by the willingness of co-partners to function as 'explorers in the borderlands' between and beyond established academic disciplines and to make good use of many of the overlapping knowledge fields. It demands sustained effort and patience, as well as the assembly of a core research team that already encompasses a variety of different backgrounds and interests – at least to the extent of knowing where to *begin* looking for solutions to emergent design problems. The issue of funding is also a pertinent one, as most university research is funded as projects lasting one to five years that are aimed at answering a specific question (or a small set of closely related questions) rather than as systematic long-term RtD programs, branching out in diverse directions from a central design core. In the case of the ESDinds project, the relative *lack* of attention paid to academic publications by funders – in contrast to the central focus on 'research for the benefit of CSOs' – may, paradoxically, have contributed towards the emergence of our design-centred post-disciplinary approach. This is because we, as participating academics, after completing the one required publication in the core field of Education for Sustainable Development and reaching the end of the funding period, were left with the nagging feeling that much more remained to be learnt and shared from the multiple unanswered questions. A combination of fortuitous circumstances, strong commitment, creative thinking and high-level institutional support were still necessary in order to translate an isolated two-year RtD initiative into a long-term post-disciplinary research agenda, which has already endured for some years since the end of the official grant period.

Despite demonstrating that it is possible for researchers to achieve this through their own efforts, we would argue that the onus is on the funders of research – both public and private – to play the leading role in facilitating design-centred post-disciplinarity, and the corresponding transformation of academia. This could be achieved by designing funding schemes that promote the longer-term systematisation of RtD, and subsequently by encouraging co-initiated and co-designed applications to these schemes from innovative community-university partnerships. While achievable in principle, this would require the abandonment of current mindsets that primarily reward short-term thinking, immediately, based on tangible outputs that assume the superior 'expertise' of the academy over community-based lived experiences. Because our approach emerged out of feedback from participants, and was not framed by any specific research paradigm, it would also be interesting to review current theoretical frameworks used in this field; for critical and creative exchange, for constructive interdisciplinary working, and for accessing potentially rich sources of new knowledge at the overlaps, gaps and inconsistencies between and across different conceptual frameworks.

Finally, we suggest that our project also highlights two issues that are emerging as particularly problematic within the current research through design literature. The first is the definition of RtD, and specifically the widespread misuse of the term 'research through design' to refer to *any* publicly disseminated and peer-reviewed design work that produces and embodies tacit knowledge (van de Weijer *et al.* 2014). As highlighted by Cross (1999) the criteria for describing an activity as 'research' are that it should address well-defined and appropriate questions; build on earlier research; adopt a methodical and systematic approach; and generate explicit and communicable knowledge, reporting results which are testable and accessible by others.

The second problematic issue relates to the assessment of quality in RtD. In addition to meeting Cross's minimum criteria to qualify as true research, it has been widely recognised that – as outlined previously – an essential quality criterion for RtD work is 'relevance', and that it should contribute both to a body of theoretical knowledge and to the advancement of practice. However, as RtD is fundamentally an interdisciplinary activity (Zimmerman *et al.* 2007), its respective contributions to knowledge and practice need to be problematized, with both 'contributions to knowledges' (in the sense of bodies of theoretical knowledge) and 'contributions to practices' understood in the plural rather than the singular. It should also be noted that the category 'practices' may refer not only to the evolution of *design* practice, but also the role of designed artefacts in transforming the day-to-day professional practice(s) of their users.

Our hope is that this project contributes iteratively to multiple knowledges and practices, and thus provides an example of best practice that uses a systematic and rigorous, but also participatory and open-ended approach, crucially focused on developing new knowledges that can be applicable more widely. We started from RtD, because the project involved the negotiation and crossing of so many disciplinary boundaries. Yet by staying firmly within design and keeping the pragmatic goal of designing usable indicators assessment tools and participatory processes at the heart of the research agenda, we were able to view other paradigms from this centre point and identify synergies between them that might otherwise have been overlooked. By systematically trying to understand phenomena with respect to our central design question, but also re-examining that question through the lens of other disciplines, we were able to build up a weft of interconnections between our work and many different fields, which illustrates just how valuable 'proper' research through design approaches can be.

In addition, throughout this book we have illustrated how collaboration and co-design have been a central element of the project from the outset. For us, working equally across a range of different partners has been crucial to generating, prototyping and iteratively improving our processes, informed by our interpretations of RtD. The initial design of the project was very innovative in terms of the role given to civil society organisation partners within the Consortium. This led to several challenges, especially administrative and financial, at the outset of the project. The social implications of this initial project design are apparent: the project is challenging the vision of research institutions as the experts and CSOs as the 'receivers' by recognising that both types of partners have expertise, albeit in different areas.

Co-design has also had an important impact on the project outcomes. While partner research institutions have focused on making the research process as rigorous as possible, input from CSO partners has been crucial in order to make sure that the project outputs were as useful as possible, before even going into the field. This focus on the usefulness of project outputs has also meant that these have been more ambitious than originally intended. This led, for example, to a repeat visit to the University of Guanajuato, Mexico, in a subsequent phase, in an effort to test whether the indicators could be applied at an institutional level, but also to enable the organisation to continue doing the evaluation 'on their own'.

In addition, the highly collaborative nature of the project and deep engagement of all consortium partners also has important social implications. One of the project partners, the European Bahá'í Business Forum (EBBF), decided to employ their own project manager after the completion of the original EU-funded work, dedicating organisational resources which will provide the opportunity for their member organisations to continue to use and further develop the values-based evaluation systems we developed. Furthermore, the deep involvement of the consortium member from the Earth Charter Initiative (ECI) has led the organisation to acquire the capacity to advise their affiliates on using the values-based indicators and assessment tools, and become committed to using them with their affiliates and related projects. ECI's full participation in the project also led their representative in the Consortium to trial the indicators with the Earth Charter's online course, e-GLO, which involves over 20 participants from all over the globe. Thus, the implications of this engagement from both ECI and EBBF are potentially huge as both are umbrella organisations that can directly influence projects and business practices around the world: ECI affiliates, youth groups and projects are present in over 80 countries and EBBF have 20 national representatives in key areas across Europe and the USA, and over 600 individual members (ECI Annual Report 2009; EBBF Annual Report 2009).

This focus on co-design and collaboration has also been underpinned by a commitment to diversity. This has been important in several ways. First, this means that the project has had input from a variety of individuals with different social and cultural backgrounds. At each Consortium General Meeting (CGM), the group openly discussed issues of faith and gender balance occurring in the project implementation and design. The Consortium did not identify any instances of discrimination, faith-imbalance or gender issues to date. In addition, the mixture of researchers' backgrounds was important in terms of research design and implementation. Although the primary data collection may have some European bias due to the nature of the project, data was collected from people from broad cultural and faith backgrounds, and several individuals from projects across the world were interviewed. Further, this diversity meant that the identification and development of indicators were not limited by the assumptions of one faith or culture. The ESDinds consortium agreed that the indicators developed thus far were faith neutral, although possibly over-leaning toward secular, and that testing them in a faith context as well as different cultural contexts would be important in order to see if they are more widely relevant.

Furthermore, the consortium actively sought to include as many socially and culturally diverse groups as possible in the field visits. In the first field phase, four out of the five organisations visited were youth groups, so the focus in the second field phase (as evidenced by the case studies in this book) shifted to businesses, larger organisations and groups involving adults rather than youth. The cultural and social diversity within the Consortium has also facilitated field visits to be carried out in linguistically and culturally diverse settings; projects visited to date were based in Germany, Luxemburg, Hungary, Austria, Italy, Switzerland, Mexico and Sierra Leone.

Through these processes, the project continues to build a community of practice, bringing together people from all fields, academic and non-academic. This has been through publication, events and by expanding networks.

Making values central: towards an ethics and societal impact

We began this book by outlining the problems for individuals, organizations and society of only having a very limited range of mechanisms for judging the effectiveness of social projects, especially where these are underpinned by important ethical and other intangible social values. We suggested that this has resulted in the deep frustration of not being able to assess the things that are most centrally important; things that are commonly related to higher human values such as integrity, trust, respect, equality and social justice; and the problematic disconnect this produces between what such individuals and organizations are trying to do, and the way this had to be articulated in funding bids and evaluation data, and even in presentation of the work to the wider public.

We hope that we have shown that it is possible to make shared social values – and their measurement – central to decisions about improving civil society; and that whilst the shared values of different groups may appear vague, intangible and difficult to explain, we can in fact offer ways of eliciting and validating them at the local level that can capture people's shared meanings across multiple goals and perspectives. Not only that, but whilst maintaining a strong and vital local validity, there are ways of capturing, measuring and communicating intangible values that are scalable, transferable and comparable across different kinds of organizations and fields of activity. What is more, engagement with the process can, in turn, have transformative impacts, both within a group and beyond it. We hope others – such as researchers, educators, civil society organisations, policy makers, funders, businesses who want to become more ethical and sustainable, professional and cross-disciplinary groupings – will make use of our approach, not merely to copy it but to take it forward into new iterations and uses.

Finally, it should be remembered that our original focus was on sustainable development, informed by the United Nations 2030 Agenda for Sustainable Development, which highlights the importance of developing new measures of progress at societal levels – rather than relying on gross domestic product (GDP) as the sole indicator. In responding to this challenge, this project, together with its partners and like-minded people and organizations, ultimately aims to be part of the strongly emerging global movements focused on how to put shared intangible social values at the centre of both discourse and action, and how to have appropriate value-based but also rigorous methods for enabling sustainable and social change.

References

Cross, N. (1999) 'Design Research: A Disciplined Conversation', *Design Issues*, 15(2), Summer, pp. 5–10.

Manzini, E. (2010) 'New Design Knowledge', *Design Studies*, 30, pp. 4–12.

van de Weijer, M., Van Cleempoel, K., and Heynen, H. (2014) 'Positioning Research and Design in Academia and Practice: A Contribution to a Continuing Debate', *Design Issues*, 30(2) Spring.

Zimmerman, J., Forlizzi, J., and Evenson, S. (2007) 'Research Through Design as a Method for Interaction Design in Human-Computer Interaction'. In *Conference on Human Factors in Computing Systems*. New York: ACM Press.

Appendix

Set 1 Sustainable Development Indicators (SDIs)

In these tables, indicators are given colour names. Red: not tested in field trials at all. Yellow: new variations that arose as a result of the field trials. Green: entirely new indicators that were suggested by participating CSOs during the field trials. Italics indicate words and phrases added during field trials. Indicators designated as headings (H…) are in shown bold type, and sub-headings (SH…) in normal type.

Set 1 Indicators for 'Justice'

Code	Indicator	Column Colour
J_H1	People feel they are treated equitably and with fairness	
J_H1'	People are treated equitably and with fairness	Yellow
J_SH1a	Individuals in a team/organization feel they have an equal opportunity to voice their opinions and their opinions are respected and listened to	
J_SH1b	Opportunities exist for all to contribute their knowledge, talents and capacities and all contributions are valued	
J_SH1c	Entities act in a manner that is impartial and non-discriminatory (not discriminating on the basis of race, colour, sex, sexual orientation, creed, religion, national or ethnic origin).	
J_H2	Ethical values of justice guide decision-making	Red
J_SH2a	People/organizations participate actively in making decisions about issues that affect their lives	
J_SH2b	Decision-making processes are ethical and democratic, transparent and provide for equal representation	
J_SH2c	Decisions take into account the social, economic and environmental needs of future generations	Red

Set 1 Indicators for 'Empowerment'

Code	Indicator	Column Colour
E_H1	People/partners become aware of how their existing knowledge, skills, networks, resources, and traditions can contribute to the project/organization/team. *Their contribution is encouraged, and people/partners feel that their talents, ideas and skills have contributed to the outcomes of the project/organization/team.*	
E_SH1a	The organization/team aims to provide all, especially children and youth, with educational opportunities that empower them to contribute actively to sustainable development.	
E_SH1b	Individuals feel they are encouraged to reach their potential, and are provided with opportunities for personal growth.	
E_SH1b'	Individuals are encouraged to reach their potential, and are provided with opportunities for personal growth.	Yellow
E_SH1b"	Individuals feel they are encouraged to reach their potential.	Yellow
E_SH1b"'	Individuals feel they are provided with opportunities for personal growth.	Yellow
E_SH1c	Individuals/Partners develop programs and deliver solutions on their own, and have a sense of power that they can effect change.	
E_H2	Members/participants contribute in a positive way to society.	Red
E_SH2a	Work is viewed as a form of service *to the wellbeing and prosperity of all creation.*	
E_H3	People/teams/organizations are given autonomy and trust to fulfil responsibilities, at the same time receiving encouragement and support.	
E_SH3a	People are not afraid to make mistakes, knowing mistakes are understood as opportunities to learn and improve.	
E_SH3b	Everyone knows what their responsibility is within the team/organization, and feels responsibility for their part of the work.	
E_H4	People/partners are encouraged to express their opinion.	
E_SH4a	People/team/partners are given the opportunity to explore and reflect upon their own ideas and traditions, and then to develop their own vision and goals for the project.	
E_SH4a	People/team/partners are taking the opportunity to explore and reflect upon their own ideas and traditions, and then to develop their own vision and goals for the project.	Yellow
E_SH4b	People/team/partners have identified their own responses to an issue, rather than just agreeing with the ideas of others.	
E_H5	In order to inspire others, individuals, leaders and organizations act as living representatives of the principles they espouse.	
E_H6	The original project has been replicated in other communities or organizations.	Red

Set 1 Indicators for 'Integrity'

Code	Indicator	Column Colour
I_H1	Ethical values and principles are used by individuals/team/organization in guiding decision-making and activities	
I_SH1a	Individuals/organization/partners conduct their activities according to principles of universal responsibility.	Red
I_SH1b	Individuals/organization/partners conduct their activities according to principles of interdependence.	
I_SH1c	Individuals/organization/partners conduct their activities according to principles of respect and care for the community of life.	Red
I_SH1d	Individuals/organization/partners conduct their activities according to principles of ecological integrity.	
I_SH1e	Individuals/organization/partners conduct their activities according to principles of social and economic justice.	Red
I_SH1f	Individuals/organization/partners conduct their activities according to principles of democracy.	Red
I_SH1g	Individuals/organization/partners conduct their activities according to principles of non-violence.	Red
I_SH1h	Individuals/organization/partners conduct their activities according to principles of peace.	Red
I_SBH1i	Truth-seeking, non-judgmental, confidential channels, which are trusted, are in place for individuals/teams seeking guidance on the application of ethics, reporting violations and examining violations of ethics.	Red
I_SH1j	Individual/team/organization can identify applicable ethical values in a given context.	Red
I_SH1k	Employment processes are conducted in a way that is fair to all applicants.	Red
I_SH1l	Actions of individuals, members, partners, affiliates and the organization are consistent and in harmony with the core principles promoted by the organization.	
I_SH1m	Individual/team/organization's behaviour is consistent with their words.	
I_H2	Individuals/team/organization/partners follow through on their commitments.	
I_SH2a	Financial integrity, resource use efficiency and performance goals are measured and reported publicly.	
I_SH2b	Goals are reviewed between committed parties to determine what has and has not been achieved.	
I_H3	Individuals have an attitude of learning towards their development, reflect critically on what is necessary to learn, and strive to bring their lives into accordance with ethical values.	Red
I_H3'	Individuals have an attitude of learning towards their development.	Yellow
I_H3"	Individuals reflect critically on what is necessary to learn.	Yellow
I_H3"'	Individuals strive to bring their lives into accordance with ethical values.	Yellow
I_SH3a	Individuals investigate what is right and good for themselves, rather than adopting other people's opinions.	Red

Set 1 Indicators for 'Trust/Trustworthiness'

Code	Indicator	Column Colour
T_H 1	Individual/ organization/partner is trusted to fulfil their commitments	Red
T_SH1a	Trusted partners are given flexibility to do things differently within prescribed structure.	Red
T_SH1b	Partners are trusted to satisfactorily deliver their commitments without the need for formal agreements.	Red
T_SH1c	Partners trust that each shares a commitment and willingness to collaborate for a similar vision	Red
T_H2	Individuals, colleagues, organizations, partners are perceived to be trustworthy, truthful, honest, transparent, respectful and practice integrity in their interactions with others.	Red
T_SH2a	Open dialogue exists between project partners.	
T_SH2b	Differences are resolved through dialogue in a way that produces learning and growth.	
T_SH2b'	Differences are resolved through dialogue.	Yellow
T_SH2b"	Conflict solving produces learning and growth.	Yellow
T_SH2c	Partners feel that their worth and value has been acknowledged. Red	
T_H3	The organization is transparent about the process and outcomes of decision-making, openly sharing information with employees.	
T_H3'	The organization is transparent about the process and outcomes of decision-making, openly sharing information with people.	Yellow
T_SH3a	Trust in people's capacities leads to active participation.	Red
T_H4	Individuals/partners/organization live the values they promote.	

Set 1 Indicators for 'Unity in Diversity'

Code	Indicator	Column Colour
U_H1	Partners, member organizations and individuals do not feel that they have compromised their beliefs by participating in the vision and activities of the organization/project.	
U_SH1a	Different points of view are heard and incorporated.	
U_SH1b	Degree to which members/partners feel that their individual identity and approach has been respected.	
U_SH1c	People are encouraged to reach their potential.	
U_H2	Everyone has his/her place in the team. Teams include members with different characteristics (e.g. gender, culture, age and other aspects of individual difference such as personality).	
U_H2'	Everyone has his/her place in the team.	Yellow
U_H2"	Teams include members with different characteristics (e.g. gender, culture, age and other aspects of individual difference such as personality).	Yellow
U_SH2a	Learning processes accommodate different learning styles.	
U_SH2b	Individuals have a feeling of a unified work environment.	
U_SH2c	Individuals learn together, share skills, abilities and information freely with one another regardless of creed, colour, ethnicity, gender.	
U_SH2d	Members are inclusive (talk to everyone and no one is left out).	
U_SH2e	Group norms exist. People follow the group norms.	
U_SH2f	Women believe they are valued.	
U_SH2g	Individuals have a feeling of harmony and pleasant work environment.	Green
U_SH2h	Everyone knows what the final goal of his/her work is, as well as the work of the whole organization.	Green
U_H3	People feel they create something better/greater as a group than on their own.	

Set 1 Indicators for 'Respect and Care for the Community of Life'

N.B. The value of Respect and Care for the Community of Life was added at CGM2 in response to concerns, especially from ECI, that the Set 1 Indicators focused almost exclusively on human interpersonal relationships at the expense of humanity's relationship with the wider community of life. Due to the time-scale of the project, this set of draft indicators could not be subjected to a process of prioritisation by the CSO partners before the field testing phase. Thus, there are 79 Set 1 Indicators in this value category (in contrast to the other values, which all had fewer than 25 Set 1 Indicators after prioritisation). The majority of these could not be field tested.

Set 1 Indicators for 'Respect and Care for the Community of Life'

Code	Draft indicator	Column Colour
3001	People treat each other with kindness, respect, equity, fairness and courtesy.	
3002	People feel that the opinion and contribution of every individual is encouraged and respected.	
3003	People feel that their individual needs for development in the work place are met.	Red
3004	People do not back-bite about people within the entity or outside the entity.	Red
3005	Regular monitoring of how people are treated and corresponding action taken to improve how people are treated.	Red
3006	Human resource management, remuneration/payment and hiring policies are fair and ensure the dignity and respect of all employees in the organization, clients and partners.	Red
3007	People are productive, loyal and creative.	Red
3008	Number of sick days (over time).	Red
3009	Number of undesired resignations.	Red
3010	People feel that their individual needs for development in the work place are met.	Red
3011	The work environment is supportive of people being able to act with care and fulfil their responsibilities in their families and personal relationships.	Red
3012	Organization uses principles of social justice to guide its activities in relation to stakeholder communities.	Red
3013	People feel that their worth and contribution is acknowledged, appreciated and valued.	
3014	People feel that there is transparent communication and the right information flow.	Red
3015	Entities are willing to work with each other because they respect each other.	Red
3016	A code of ethics is developed with employees, as well as the procedures to deal with unethical conduct.	Red
3017	There is a safe environment for people in the entity's activities.	Red
3018	Entity respects and acknowledges the contributions of others to their work, and gives credit for the outcomes to those who contributed.	Red
3019	There is a culture of learning and encouragement.	Red
3020	People are not afraid to make mistakes.	Red
3021	Individuals have self-respect.	Red
3022	Individuals strive to become conscious of their value system and put their values into practice.	Red
3023	People accept and appreciate the differences in other people and find a way to understand them.	Red
3024	Organization/individuals show respect for and understanding of diverse points of view, beliefs, and traditions in their work and in decision-making.	Red
3025	Degree to which individuals/partners learn about and/or understand each other's traditions.	Red

Code	Draft indicator	Column Colour
3026	Individuals/partners feel that they have been given the opportunity to explore the wisdoms, traditions and values that they already hold, rather than having something imposed upon them.	Red
3027	Staff within an organization feels that different approaches and ideas are valued and respected.	Red
3028	Degree to which individuals/partners feel that their individuality is respected, and difference is recognized.	Red
3029	Degree to which individuals/partners are willing to listen to or appreciate different ideas or opinions.	Red
3030	Degree to which individuals/partners are able to suspend their own values or ideas and listen to those of others.	Red
3031	Organization allows local groups, who have an interest in their work, to contribute their ideas or become partners on a project.	Red
3032	Decision-making and consultative processes in the organization are carried out with respect, honesty and fairness.	Red
3033	Decisions made in the organization are supported.	Red
3034	Ideas are introduced to each other with respect, modesty and patience.	Red
3035	Entity/initiative strives to have a positive effect on the natural environment.	Red
3036	Environmental sustainability is a principle applied during decision-making.	Red
3037	Purchasing policy requires the exclusive use of recycled paper.	Red
3038	Proportion of paper used that is recycled.	Red
3039	Long term commitments to protect the environment are created and adhered to.	
3040	Celebrations within an organization /community are conducted in an environmentally friendly manner.	Red
3041	Ecological footprint.	Red
3042	Ratio of the use of resources by the organization over a fair allocation of resources.	Red
3043	Proportion of energy used that is renewable.	Red
3044	The organization strives to sell products that have no or a positive environmental impact.	Red
3045	The organization is open to dialogue about alternative means of production that have no or a positive impact on the environment.	Red
3046	Entity actively seeks or is willing to work with others who will increase their ability to improve the environment.	Red
3047	Organization has objectives and implements strategies to reduce carbon emissions by 50% by 2050.	Red
3048	Education is undertaken to raise awareness and capabilities for the organization to act according to principles of environmental sustainability.	Red
3049	Proportion of investment in initiatives that are environmentally sustainable as compared to those that are not.	Red

Code	Draft indicator	Column Colour
3050	Entity is aware of their environmental impact and contribution to environmental problems and takes responsibility for their actions acting to reduce or remedy it.	Red
3051	Organization/community/individual has successfully reduced environmental impact.	Red
3052	Entity has zero or positive impact on the natural environment.	Red
3053	Entity feels compelled to protect environment and do not wait for governments or other to take action prior to acting themselves.	
3054	Entity recognises their role as a protector of nature.	Red
3055	Number of activities/projects towards goal of environmental sustainability.	Red
3056	Quality of process and results of activities or projects aiming to achieve or promote environmental sustainability.	
3057	The environment and community of life is celebrated.	
3058	Activities initiated and completed in the conscious aim of contributing to a greater respect for nature.	
3059	Activities initiated and completed in the conscious aim of contributing to a greater understanding and respect of how nature is organized (systems and cycles).	
3060	Activities initiated and completed in the conscious aim of contributing to a greater valuing of the natural world as a source of personal fulfilment.	
3061	Activities initiated and completed in the conscious aim of making the Earth healthy and beautiful for future children (e.g. children think that the earth is healthier and more beautiful as a result of their activity).	Red
3062	Activities initiated and completed to protect and restore the web of life.	Red
3063	Activities initiated and completed that share with others how to protect and restore the Earth's health.	
3064	Members of a faith are aware of the connectedness between their religion and the environment.	Red
3065	Amount of environmental education programs undertaken within local schools.	Red
3066	Number of activities/projects for raising awareness of environmental sustainability.	Red
3067	Quality of process and results of activities or projects aiming to achieve or promote social aspects of sustainability.	Red
3068	Entity contributes positively to society by working to address social problems and global issues.	Red
3069	Number of activities/projects towards goal of addressing the social aspects of sustainability.	Red
3070	Number of activities/projects for raising awareness of social aspects of sustainability.	Red
3071	Degree to which participants consciously espouse the values of care and respect.	Red
3072	The project's activities/events have an emotional effect on participants.	

Code	Draft indicator	Column Colour
3073	The project's messages/activities trigger in others new personal and organizational initiatives that improve the world/planet.	Red
3074	Values and lifestyles change as a result of participation in the project's activities. The lifestyle is more sustainable, includes more conscious pro-environmental behaviours (environmentally significant in sustainable way).	Red
3075	Level of personal investment (time, finances, social) by participants in activities that benefit the world/planet.	Red
3076	Entities develop attitudes and capabilities for principled action.	Red
3077	Participants/people have respect for nature.	Red
3078	Environmental knowledge: Participants/people understand how complex nature systems are.	Red
3079	Participants/people valuate natural world as a source personal fulfilment.	Red
3080	Entity is aware of the interconnectedness between the environment and their sphere of activity.	Red

Index